To God be the glory —
Dixie Parker

DO NOT ASK WHY;
Only Trust

D1009069

Written by

DIXIE PARKER

www.xulonpress.com

I dedicate this book to my family and all those who
have walked beside me on my journey

TABLE OF CONTENTS

INTRODUCTION

As I walked through the doorway into the small concrete block home, my eyes squinted as they adjusted from the sunlight outside to the darkened atmosphere. My eyes slowly surveyed the trash and dirty clothes piled high in the corners of the room. I had visited the house before and had become friends with the woman who lived there, but today I was on a special mission.

Today, I had come to see her new baby. As I greeted my friend, I heard a rustling below me, and as I peered downward, I saw the little baby. It was difficult for my mind to grasp what I was seeing as I saw the newborn baby lying on the concrete floor in a cardboard box. I saw that she lay in a diarrhea-dried blanket. As I reached down to pick her up, the roaches that were hiding under her small body scattered within the box.

When I later walked into the kitchen, my eyes were directed to what was lying under the kitchen table. Over the months since Christmas, the rats had cleaned every morsel off the turkey carcass that had been carelessly thrown onto the floor.

I wondered, "How in the world did I get here?" It was all I could do to comprehend and accept this kind of poverty. Two years earlier, I would not have believed that anyone lived in these conditions.

How did I get from living in a ten-room country home to working in the inner city in Lexington, Kentucky?

The path of life led me through times of sorrow, as I dealt with my husband's death, to times of joy as I watched God answer prayer and provide a 33,000-square-foot building that became known as Christ Center.

My own personal journey took me down many bends and unexpected turns on the road of life.

Most people's stories tell of their lives going from "rags to riches," but I went from having every-thing I wanted to dependence on God to provide our next meal.

This book is about my life and the lessons I learned along the way. But, more than that, this book is about the faithfulness of God, how He meets ordi-nary people during the different seasons of their lives, and how He answers prayer.

Jim wanted me to write our story so that the gen-erations that follow us, our children, grandchildren, and great-grandchildren would have the account of our lives after God apprehended our hearts.

Chapter One

SEASON OF NEW BEGINNINGS

Romans 5:8, "But God demonstrates his own love for us in this: While we were still sinners, Christ died for us."

Eighty-Six Shirts & Thirteen Suits

*P*onytails and poodle skirts still bring back memories of dancing at the Gym Jams at the local YMCA, walking home hand-in-hand with my date, and other fun times I had while living in a small town in the Ohio Valley in the 1950s. I met and fell in love with a handsome young man named Galen Bebout. At the beginning of our relationship, life was like a fairy tale. Galen and I lived in small towns about thirty miles apart in Ohio. Galen's parents were wealthy, and he lived a life of surreal indulgence, while I was from a typical middle class family.

During one visit to his home, I remember counting eighty-six shirts in his closet as well as thirteen suits. I couldn't even begin to imagine someone having that many clothes! At that time, I was working in a bakery and would have to save my money for weeks if I wanted something special like a pair of pedal pushers or whatever the latest fad was. When we would go on a date with other couples, Galen always paid the bill at the restaurant and was a very giving person. He was extremely handsome, generous, easy to get along with and easy to love.

Soon, we were engaged, and Galen showered me with gifts. In the year we were engaged, the week before Christmas, I mentioned that I had seen a fur blend sweater I loved and was going to save to buy it. On Christmas Eve, Galen came to my home with a hope chest for my Christmas present. When I opened the chest, I discovered that it was filled with fur blend sweaters. Galen told me that he went to the store where I saw the sweater and bought me one of every color that was in my size.

When we were married, we moved into a ten-room home in the country that his father had given us. The house had a large kitchen with hardwood flooring that was around twelve feet by twenty-two feet. Besides the kitchen, there was a dining room and den, plus two living rooms on the first floor, so we set up a bedroom in the den and just lived in the downstairs. I didn't know what to do with the mudroom off the kitchen that my mother-in-law had used when she had horses. I was so young that I would just shut the doors of the rooms that I couldn't relate too. The bedrooms upstairs sat untouched. The downstairs of the house was larger than the two-story house in which I had lived while in high school.

I didn't know how to cook or how to clean a house. One of our friends would always tease me about a situation that happened the first year of my marriage:

My television was broken, so I called the TV repairman, who knew Galen. When he came to fix the TV, I was trying to clean house. I had decided to vacuum the couch in the living room where the television was. As the repairman was behind the TV doing this repair, he saw me trying to vacuum the sofa. The only trouble was that I had all of the attachments hooked together and was six feet from the couch, trying to vacuum it! He was laughing so hard that he couldn't come out from behind the TV because I would see him laughing at me.

I was so homesick during the first year of my marriage, many days I would be crying. On these occasions, I would take a bath when Galen was supposed to arrive home from work so that he wouldn't see my red face and know that I had been weeping from my loneliness. For the first six months that we lived out in the country, I didn't know anyone, I didn't have a car to drive, and I felt more like a prisoner than the princess that Galen treated me like. All I had was this big house that I didn't know how to take care of. It was full of beautiful furniture, but at eighteen years of age, I didn't appreciate much of what I had. I felt more like a trophy for Galen than his wife.

Is This A Nightclub?

The biggest disaster we had while living in the big house came on New Year's Eve. We had decided to have a New Year's Eve party, so I invited my friends from my hometown, and he invited his friends. We made preparations for thirty people to attend our party. Galen had already done too much celebrating before our guests arrived, so shortly after the party started, he went upstairs and went to bed, leaving me to do the entertaining. About 100 people showed up during the first few hours of the party. I was shocked when two couples who I did not know came up to me around midnight and asked me where to buy the drinks. They told me they had stopped because they thought the house was a nightclub from all the cars parked on the lawn.

It was raining that night, and by morning the grass and circle driveway in front of the house was full of mud ruts from all the cars. Whiskey bottles were carelessly thrown over the yard, and all the rooms upstairs were filled with people who had passed out or just gone to sleep during the evening.

At seven o'clock the next morning, I heard a loud noise at the side entrance of our house. I had slept on the couch after the party, as all of the beds were occupied. The commotion woke me from a sound sleep. Galen's parents were standing inside our screened-in porch, loudly knocking on our kitchen door, attempting to wake someone up. The last thing I wanted to do was face them. They were visibly upset as they told me they had received several phone calls that morning, telling them about the party that had taken place.

I would have loved to have been a genie at that moment and disappear into a bottle instead of having to face them. My gaze followed theirs as they surveyed the living room and we both saw the arm of the chair that they had bought us for Christmas, lying on the floor. I was as shocked as they were when I saw the condition of the brand new chair. In a feeble attempt to lighten the mood, I nonchalantly said, "Oh, by the way, the arm fell off the chair that you gave us."

A steady stream of people came downstairs, looking disoriented with shirttails hanging out of their pants, disheveled hair, and/or partially dressed as they left. Finally, Galen came down and encountered his parents. Galen and his dad had a heated discussion, and then it was over. Galen was their only child, conceived late in life, so he usually ended up winning the arguments. They loved him dearly, but were always frustrated that they couldn't control his actions no matter how hard they tried. My father-in-law, Ken, could control most situations in his life, but he could not control this one. He would get very angry with Galen, but would then try to make it all right by trying to buy back the peace with gifts and money.

Galen worked for his dad, and if we couldn't live within his salary, he would take whatever he needed from the business. I had worked all through high school and was from a family that took responsibility seriously; I could not go along with this. Galen would buy boats and throw me the payment book to pay for them. He loved guns and was always buying or trading them for the newest design.

Galen's way of coping with what he was spending was to tell me to spend the same amount of money that he was spending. If he spent thousands on a boat, I could spend thousands on whatever I wanted. What would have happened if I had done what he said and left the results up to him? During most of our marriage, I was under a lot of financial pressure because I would not ask his family for money and was always juggling our finances. I guess that was where the words "creative financing" came from!

After almost a year, Galen got restless and decided he wanted us to buy a house in town. I didn't know he felt this way until he came home one day and told me he wanted me to see the house he had picked out for us to buy.

(It is amazing to me, as I write this, that at that time in my life, I just accepted him doing that. Times are certainly different now. These days, the idea of "teamwork" in marriage is widely taught and accepted as the healthy norm.)

God, If You're Really There!

As an adult, my first real encounter with God was over the difficulty of becoming pregnant. I tried to conceive for three years, but was not successful. Dealing with infertility was like riding an emotional roller coaster. One minute, I would feel like I was on the top of the ride and in just an instant, I would be carried to the bottom. Each month my period didn't start on time, I would be elated and think I was pregnant. Then my emotions would come crashing down when I would start my period. The moment that I would think I was expecting, I would start emotionally relating to the baby I thought I was carrying, only to be devastated when my period would eventually start.

After many painful months of failing to become pregnant, I was lying on the bed at around midnight one night, and I cried out to God. I begged, "God, if You really are there, I will make a deal with You. If You let me get pregnant, I will quit smoking."

At that point in my life, smoking was something I figured God wouldn't like, if He really did exist. That night, I did actually conceive, and nine months later we had a darling baby girl, Teri. I kept part of my bargain with God. I gave up smoking for the nine months of my pregnancy, but I started smoking again after the baby was born.

Pebbles At The Window

Galen's father wanted us to go to church. I felt that he only wanted us to attend church for show because he was a county commissioner, had a car dealership and owned several farms. I thought he wanted us to be seen at church for purely political reasons. I knew it would make him look good.

Ken reminded me of the character, "Boss Hog" on the TV series, "The Dukes of Hazard," because he was rotund in size and most of the time wore a three-piece suit. He was almost as big around as he was tall. When he would get angry, he would start poking his finger into your chest and his face would many times turn a slight purplish color. He was like a volcano ready to erupt at any time; he would get so angry that he looked like he could explode at any given moment.

One Sunday morning, Ken came over and threw pebbles at our upstairs bedroom window to wake us up. Galen sleepily opened the window and he and his dad had a heated discussion, yelling at each other. Galen and I had been out partying the night before and hadn't gotten to bed until the wee hours of the morning. Ken yelled to Galen that we needed to get up and go to church. Galen replied that he was not going and proceeded to go back to bed. At this point, Ken started throwing pebbles at the window again. There was a standoff between them, and all that I could think of was the fact that the neighbors could hear the screaming match taking place.

At that point, I said, "Let's just go, so he will leave us alone about it."

Galen and his dad's argument ended as most of them did. They would argue and shout, and after each one got off his chest how he felt, they would go about their daily business. There was never any solving or resolution to the problem they would be arguing about. The problems between Galen and his dad remained buried within themselves as land mines buried under the ground. None were visible to the eye, but were ready to explode at a later time.

Short Shorts

We finally went to church and met the new young pastor and his wife, Frank and Millie Dawson. Several months later, Frank called and asked me if I would like to help the young adult class paint the church parsonage fence. I said, "Sure," thinking that it would be a good way to get a suntan.

I noticed the strange looks on the faces of the other young adults as I pulled up in my red Edsel convertible with the top down. I was wearing short shorts and a strapless halter, with a pack of Lucky Strikes stuck down in the front of my halter. The young adults all looked at me as if the town floozy had arrived. I was just as amazed at how they were dressed. Instead of being dressed to get a suntan, they wore sweatshirts and slacks, and the only skin showing was their hands and face. Everyone avoided painting next to me except the pastor's young son, who was intrigued with the pack of cigarettes stuck in my halter front.

On the way home, I thought back over the day and how accepted I had felt by the young pastor and his wife. Frank and Millie had been very kind and loving toward me. I decided that whatever they had found in their lives was what I wanted. At the time, I did not realize that what they had was a personal relationship with Jesus Christ, the living God.

I already had a husband who loved and adored me, and had a daughter who I loved deeply, but that had not filled the void in my life that God had placed within me. The scientist Pascal has said that every person has a God-shaped vacuum in their life that only God can fill. That day, I became aware of that empty place in my life. I had always thought that something outside of myself would make me happy, but I realized that day that what I needed was something to fill the hole I felt deep within myself.

As a teenager, I thought that being popular was the way to happiness. Later on, I thought being married would make the difference. Once I was married,

I thought that having a baby was the answer. After many nights of getting up for nighttime feedings and washing dirty diapers, I realized that having a baby was not the golden ring I had been searching for in life.

I Found The Key

Several months passed, and Frank called again to ask if I would be interested in going to a church camp with some of the people from his church. I was curious about what a church camp for adults would actually be like. When I asked Frank and Millie about it, they told me that if I didn't want to go to any of the meetings, I didn't have to. They also said that there was a swimming pool at the camp. When I asked if I could smoke at camp and they said, "Yes," camp didn't seem like such a bad idea.

Galen was scheduled to be away for two weeks at National Guard Camp, and my mother said she would watch our daughter, Teri, so I decided to go for a weekend. Millie arranged for me to drive to the camp with her because Frank was going early with the other people from the church.

The first day at the camp, I didn't go to any meetings but just sat around the pool, smoking. I felt like an animal on display at a zoo as the children watched me through the metal fence that surrounded the swimming pool. The second day, I heard about a class called "Motion in Devotion," which sounded interesting. It was an exercise class done to Christian music. About 100 people were on a lawn, all of them standing about arm's length apart, when the exercise began. After about a half an hour of doing the exercises, they played a song called, "Open My Eyes." I did the motions to the song and my life changed for all eternity in that moment. I heard the words:

"Open my eyes that I may see,
 glimpses of truth thou hast for me,
 Place in my hands the wonderful key
 that shall unclasp and set me free."
(Written by Clara S. Scott, 1841-1897, Psalm 119:18)

As I sang the words, "Open my eyes," I put my hands up to my eyes and took them away. I then held my hands out in front of me while singing, "Place in my hand the wonderful key that shall unclasp and set me free." As I did these motions while singing the song, I suddenly realized that I actually meant what I was singing. On the outside, I appeared happy and content with life, but I was actually miserable inside, and I needed to be set free. I felt all locked up within myself.

People say the longest distance in the world is from your head to your heart. That day, all the things I had ever learned as a child about Jesus loving me and about His dying on the cross for my sins suddenly became alive and real. In an instant, His love and His death became reality in my life, and I have never been the same since. I started weeping as I put my hands out in front of me as if to hold the key. The key (of God's love) truly unlocked the chambers of my heart that had been closed to Him for so long.

#007 Christian

I left the camp and arrived back in Mount Vernon as a Secret Service Christian. I knew that I had become a Christian, and God knew it, but no one else did except the people at camp. I didn't tell any of our social friends for several months until I became used to the idea. Galen was very accepting of my newfound faith and even encouraged me in it. At that point in my life, I didn't know any other Christians my age who had been going my previous direction and then changed in mid-stream. I realize now that I could have used some help in maturely sorting things out — like how to act around my non-Christian friends.

At one dance, one of the men in our party got so frustrated with me that he threw a mixed drink down the front of my gold satin cocktail dress because I wouldn't drink with him as I would have in the past. He and I had been the life of the party at past dances. I am sure he must have been reacting to the judgments I was unknowingly placing on him. I only drank at dances and parties, so after three drinks, I would be game for any crazy thing. Years later, I realized that I had just as much fun *without* drinking as I did drinking. My fun personality stayed the same, sober or not, and I didn't need the added courage that alcohol gave me.

Six months after my encounter with God at camp, Galen and I were in a nightclub, watching a belly dancer with a huge jewel in her navel. I can remember thinking, "O Lord, what would You think if You came back tonight and saw me sitting here in this nightclub?"

I had to figure out how to live a Christian life with a husband who was not interested in changing his lifestyle. I began attending a Bible study on the nights that Galen had to work late, so that I could be home when he was. From then on, I would get up and take Teri to church by myself if he didn't want to go. One Sunday morning, I remember getting Teri and myself ready for church. Galen was lying in bed, talking to me as I got ready. I asked him if he would like to go with me to church.

He said, "No, you go for us all."

I replied, "Honey, you can't get to heaven on the family plan," and we both laughed.

Chapter Two

SEASON OF DISILLUSIONMENT

11 Corinthians 12:9, "My grace is sufficient for you, for my power is made perfect in weakness."

Walking the Tight Rope

Slowly, God started changing me on the inside as well as on the outside. As I would do the ironing, I would pray for God to iron the wrinkles out of my life. When I would clean the kitchen floor, I would pray for God to clean my heart of anything unclean. I loved Jesus so much for the freedom from guilt and shame that He had won for me by His death on the cross. Truly, He was a friend who met my heart's deepest longings for love and acceptance. I knew Jesus was someone who would never leave me nor forsake me.

I especially needed to know that Jesus was a faithful friend in the following years of my life, when tragedy struck my Cinderella world. During the fifth year of our marriage, Galen started having mental problems. He was eventually checked into the psychiatric ward at Riverside Hospital in Columbus, Ohio. There was much trauma during this season in my life. I slept on a cot in his room for the first week. He was in this hospital for six weeks and was then released and sent home.

His dad would not accept that Galen was having mental problems and wanted him out of the hospital. Ken put intense pressure on me to check Galen out of the hospital. He finally persuaded the doctor that Galen needed to be released, since I would not sign the release forms. I found out later that Ken was spreading rumors that I had checked Galen into a psychiatric ward at the hospital to make everyone believe that he was mentally ill so that I could try to get control of his money. He was home for two weeks, and those two weeks were living hell for us all as my husband tried to take his life four times in that period.

Galen's dad still did not want to believe that Galen was ill, but the sheriff told Ken (in my presence) that Galen had to be taken to a state hospital if his father could not find a private hospital that had a place for him. The sheriff was called when Galen made the last attempt to take his life, so the decision was taken out of his father's control. Galen was seriously ill and needed treatment that we could not give him.

He was finally sent to a very expensive private hospital. That mental hospital was supposed to be the second best hospital in the nation. It was in a town about an hour-and-a-half drive from Mount Vernon where we were living. I closed up our house and moved with Teri back to my parents in Newark during his hospital stay. I went back to work clerking at the local grocery store that I had worked in during my high school years. I had to work to make our house payments for our home in Mount Vernon as Galen's dad did not offer me any help, and I would not ask him for it.

Initially, the hospital staff told me they thought he would not recover. It is difficult to describe the emotions I went through during Galen's illness. Most people like me probably don't have a clue about coping with a loved one suffering mental illness until it is experienced first-hand. I felt many times that I was walking a tightrope high in the air, and if I made a wrong move I would plunge to the ground. I felt like a person dressed like a trapeze artist who had not been taught how to walk the tightrope, but was expected to know how to do it.

I never knew what was going to happen next. The only predictable thing in my life during that period was Jesus. He was the one who held me stable when I thought I was going to fall off the tightrope. He was my security when everything around me seemed to be falling apart.

Galen was in the hospital for only five months. He got out, I believe, as a result of answered prayer. During the time that Galen was in the hospital, I went to a small prayer group at Frank and Millie's home. I was the only young person there; most of the women were older and had gray hair. (When I shared this story while speaking at a women's retreat several years ago, I realized that I was now the age of the women I had called old. How life changes!)

One evening while I was at the prayer meeting, I asked the women to pray with me for God to give Galen a second chance. The next morning, I could hardly believe what I was hearing when a doctor from the hospital called and said that there had been an amazing change in Galen from the day before. He said Galen would be discharged in the next month.

Before Galen was released from the hospital, I went to a meeting with his parents, doctors, psychologist, and our social workers. Galen was not present at this meeting. We all sat around a large conference table facing one another. I watched his parents' faces as the doctors described what they felt would be the best plan for Galen's future. His parents were told that the best situation for Galen would be for him, Teri, and me to move far away, possibly as far away as California. They said that Galen would not be strong enough to do this without his parents' total support and encouragement.

My heart sank as I heard his mother tell the doctors that Galen was her only child and she would not do it. She went on to ask them if they would be able to do this if it meant being separated from their only child. His parents didn't seem to understand that unless Galen was in a situation to maintain normal mental health, they would not really have him anyway. They could have his physical presence, but not Galen functioning with a healthy mind. I had missed Galen so much during the five-month separation while he was in the hospital, but I wanted a healthy Galen back home, not just the essence of him. I wanted him to be able to maintain the mental health he had attained to this point. I wanted the Galen I had fallen in love with. Instead, his dad gave him a large salary increase to come back to work for him and take over the management of the car dealership.

Not long after Galen got released from the hospital, we left on a two-week vacation to Las Vegas and California. His dad was awarded the trip through the car dealership and gave us the trip. A picture of Galen and me, taken at a cocktail party in Las Vegas, appeared on the society page of our hometown newspaper. From the outside looking in, life seemed back to normal, but I was always worried about Galen's health if he ever arrived home later than expected, or if he was under pressure from his job. Life around us went on as normal, and we slowly acclimated to it and tried to be as normal as possible. For the next nine months, Galen and I drove to Columbus every two weeks for him to visit his doctor. The doctor felt that Galen was progressing in his journey and quest for mental health.

The Ticket Booth

About that time, I had a disturbing dream one night. It was a very unusual dream. In the dream, I was in a room with benches around the outer walls. There was a booth, like a movie theater ticket booth, in one corner with a woman sitting in it. Next to the booth was a door that a man would open when a number was called. A person would get up when his number was called and would walk through the door. The people sitting in the room were prostitutes, drug addicts, and other obvious sinners.

I was the only person in the room who saw beyond the door. I knew what was going to happen to them as their number was called and they went to the door. The people would get up and nonchalantly walk to the door as if it was a normal day in their lives. They had no idea what the next moment held for them. The door was on the very edge of a huge cliff that dropped into utter darkness. When a person stepped through the door, he or she would fall into the black abyss. I saw the horror on their faces as they were falling without any way to stop themselves.

I knew what would keep them from going through the door. I was walking around the room carrying Teri, and was frantically telling the people that Jesus loved them and that He had died on the cross for their sins. I was telling them about the love of Jesus with intense passion for their souls. I felt God's love for each person and His desire for each one to know Him and be saved from the utter darkness. All they had to do was accept God's plan and live life His way.

The next morning, I woke up at about six a.m. and was disturbed by my dream. I remembered every small detail and felt the passion in my heart for the people in the dream. I was concerned because Teri and I had been by ourselves. Galen wasn't in the dream at all. I called Frank and Millie Dawson and asked them if I could come to their home. By seven o'clock, I was pulling up in front of their home with Teri. I shared my dream with Frank and Millie and asked them if they knew what it meant. Frank gave me a very wise answer. He told me if the dream was from God, it would come true. If the dream wasn't from God, I should not worry about it but just trust the Lord. With that reply, I committed my dream to God and went on with my life.

A few years later, when I was witnessing to prostitutes and drug addicts on the streets in Lexington's inner city, I remembered my dream. It was then that I realized I was feeling the same passion for lost souls that I had felt in my dream.

Smell of Gun Powder

Galen was home from the hospital for nine months before he died. Two weeks before Galen took his life, the psychiatrist who treated Galen at the hospital released him as clinically healed and well. The psychiatrist said we didn't have to make any more trips every two weeks for counseling.

The night that Galen took his life, I called the psychiatrist and told him what had happened. The psychiatrist wept on the phone. He said that out of the 2,000 patients he had treated, Galen was the last one he thought would ever take his life.

It is hard to describe the trauma I went through the evening that Galen committed suicide. We had packed the car to leave on vacation the next morning with our two closest friends. Galen and I had been upstairs, dressing to go out with another couple for the evening. I heard the doorbell ring and went down to answer it. As I opened the front door, I heard a gun fire. As I ran upstairs, the smell of gunpowder filled the air. It permeated my entire being and I was engulfed in it. I ran into the bedroom and saw Galen lying on the floor with a fatal gunshot wound in the head. Nothing in life could prepare me for a moment like that.

I was in shock as I ran down the stairs to call an ambulance. It was hard for me to comprehend what was happening. My friend who had just arrived had to help me dial the number because I was shaking so badly. At first I couldn't even get the phone right-side up in my hand. Inside myself I was screaming, "Help me, help me, somebody help me." Outwardly, I was only shaking, but inside I was falling apart and couldn't pull the pieces back together.

My friend's husband ran upstairs and realized that Galen was already dead. I remember that someone took me next door. The babysitter took Teri to a neighbor's home to protect Teri from the trauma of the death of her daddy.

I can remember the helplessness I felt sitting in the neighbor's living room, trying to comprehend all that had happened that evening. I felt like I was in a dream. My life fell apart the instant Galen pulled the trigger on the gun. Frank Dawson, my pastor, arrived at our neighbor's home a short time later. Frank helped me learn a lesson that kept me from going into a reaction of complete hopelessness. That evening, Frank told me I shouldn't ask God why Galen had killed himself, but that I needed to trust God.

I took what Frank told me to heart, but it was a process that took until the early hours of the morning to fully grasp. Teri and I spent the night at our friend's house, since my parents lived in another town, and I wanted to stay close by. I remember sitting up most of the night in a recliner in their living room. I couldn't sleep. My thoughts felt like vultures swirling over my head, waiting to swoop down and devour me. I felt like the darkness was trying to swallow me. Vultures of despair, rejection, hopelessness, loneliness, and grief — all the emotions one would feel in the situation stalked me as their prey.

I was a whirlwind of thoughts and emotions. I felt rejection—why had Galen chosen to kill himself rather than being willing to work out whatever problem seemed so insurmountable to living? I feared being left alone to raise our child, of being a single mom. I felt a deep guilt—had I said or done something wrong? Was I to blame? Could I have done something to keep him from killing himself? Had I not been what he needed as a wife?

By morning, I had fought off the vultures and had come to the conclusion that Frank was right. I did not need to ask God why this happened, but I needed to choose to trust Him. After wrestling with my thoughts all night long, I was no closer to answering *why* than when I first started asking myself the questions. With the rising of the sun, I saw clearly what Frank had told me the night before and threw myself on the mercy of God to help me through the difficult times ahead.

I realized the only answer I was ever going to find was that I could not figure it all out, but simply had to trust God. I did not have to know why it had happened. Over the months, I realized I could not have done anything differently to change the outcome, and I could not have kept it from happening.

One of the lessons I learned along the way is that tragedy happens to many people, and most of the time there aren't any answers to explain why they occur. When faced with a tragedy, some people choose to ask, "Why, why, why did this happen to me?" At the end of asking the question, they are no closer to answers than when they started asking. Asking *why* about tragedy is a vicious cycle, a bottomless pit for those who go that direction, because it only leads to more despair.

I will never know why Galen chose to end his life, or why it happened to me. I was twenty-four years old, with a three-year-old daughter, and I was left without a husband. My daughter was left without a daddy. At that time, I chose to believe that God knew everything and loved me; that I didn't have to understand it and probably never would. Some situations in life can never be explained or understood, no matter how long and hard we think about them. But with the help of God, we can live through them and become survivors.

Trusting God and accepting Galen's death did not mean I bypassed the times of heartache and mourning. I mourned the loss of the one I loved. I mourned the loss of the future with the one I loved. I mourned the "what could have been," the love unfulfilled. The pain I felt was both emotional and physical. During the times of intense weeping, I felt as if my heart was physically breaking into pieces. During these times of weeping, I would imagine Jesus holding me in His arms as I wept. He knew my pain.

Years later, I realized the adjustments Mom and Dad made in their lives while Teri and I lived with them. Teri and I ate dinner most evenings with them, and many mornings Mom would bring a pot of coffee upstairs if I didn't go down to visit her. Mom and Dad put their social lives on hold to be there for Teri and me. They taught me about loving and caring for adult children without ever saying a word. Their lives were an example of love full of unspoken words. God provided His love for Teri and me through my parents' love. Theirs were the arms that held us when we were hurting and wiped away our tears. Their love helped fill some of the empty spaces that Galen's death had left within us.

Unknown Valleys

After Galen's death, I sold our home in Mount. Vernon, Ohio, and moved to Newark, Ohio, where my parents lived. They had bought the old Worley mansion that had been built around the turn of the century. Mom and Dad worked many long hours restoring the house. It had fifteen rooms in the main house, plus an apartment over the garage that had been the caretaker's quarters, as well as an apartment on the third floor that had been the maid's quarters. Teri and I moved into the third-floor apartment.

I made a lot of mistakes during this season of my life, as I learned to adjust to loss and as I tried to cope with Galen's death. I had to deal with the feelings of rejection that I felt from Galen taking his life instead of choosing life and working out the dark night of the soul that he must have faced within himself. I faced my own dark night of the soul during this time, but it is through these dark, unknown valleys that we learn the most about God and His love for us.

Reflections

The Bible says that God doesn't give us more than we can handle and in 2 Corinthians 12:9, it states, "My grace is sufficient for you, for my power is made perfect in weakness." Through the following months, I learned the reality and truth of these scriptures.

I have realized that we all go through a season of disillusionment at some time in our lifetime, as life never unfolds the way that we plan. We enter a marriage not expecting tragedy, either from a death or the death of a marriage through divorce. We have children, not expecting our darling 'wee ones' to rebel when they become teenagers. We get diseases and illnesses when we thought, in our youth, that we would always have healthy bodies. For some, it is the disillusionment that having money and possessions will meet their inner needs for acceptance and happiness.

The challenge we face is to believe that God loves us in the midst of facing our disenchantments. It is easier to feel God's love when our present reality is happiness and spontaneous joy.

God, help us to trust Your care for us when we are traveling through a season of disillusionment.

Chapter Three

SEASON OF A LOVE FULFILLED

Psalm 36:4-5, "Delight yourself in the Lord and he will give you the desires of your heart. Commit your way to the Lord, trust in him and he will do this:"

God's Master Plan

It is still amazing to me to reflect on how God directed my path, how I met my future husband, Jim Parker, and how I got to Wilmore, Kentucky. I believe God has a master plan for each one of our lives. As we seek Him and follow His guidance, God works it all out for His purposes.

Frank and Millie Dawson were going to Wilmore, Kentucky, during the Memorial Day weekend to attend the Asbury College graduation. They invited me to go with them. I had never been to a Christian college and hadn't even thought of going away to school, but Frank and Millie had thought about it. We drove for six hours from Gambier, Ohio, to Wilmore, Kentucky. Wilmore is a small town nestled in the green rolling hills of the countryside. Limestone fences that were built by slaves before the Civil War surround beautiful horse farms. The fences are about four feet tall with flat stone laid upon flat stone. They did not use any mortar or material between the stones to hold them in place, but were expertly fitted together and are still standing. The town is small but swells in size during the school year as students fill the dorms at the college and seminary. Asbury College sits on one side of the main street in town, and the seminary is located on the opposite side of the street. Large red brick colonial buildings with tall white pillars line the half-circle driveway as you arrive at the college. We went to the college cafeteria to have lunch as soon as we arrived.

While we were eating, Frank said, "Why don't we go to the dean's office? I know Dean Pike. Let's see if there is any possibility of you going to school here this fall."

I went with Frank, not really thinking of moving to Wilmore to go to school because I had a four-year-old daughter and had been comfortable living with my parents after Galen's death. Frank and I walked over to the administration building and into the dean's office. Frank asked if Dean Pike was in his office. The receptionist said that he wasn't.

I thought, "Well, God has closed that door."

As we turned to leave, I walked out the door first and ran right into an elderly gentleman who was

35

carrying a huge pile of papers. The papers instantly flew out of his arms, and papers fell like snow all over the office and hallway. I was so totally embarrassed. I quickly stooped over to pick up the papers for the startled gentleman.

Frank said, "Dixie, I would like to introduce you to Dean Pike." He then told Dean Pike who I was. He said that I was a young widow from his church who had a four-year-old daughter and was thinking about going to college.

The dean asked me if I had been to college before and what was my grade point average. I told him that I had gone to night school in Newark, Ohio, at the Ohio State University Branch after my husband's death. I had only taken one course in history, but had gotten a 3.8 grade point average. Dean Pike said that if I could find a place to live, he would let me attend Asbury College that fall. I was shocked that he said he would admit me without even seeing my transcript. It was very unusual to be accepted into a private college for the fall quarter when it was already the end of May.

Next, Frank and I went down the hall to the office of the person who was in charge of housing on campus. Frank knew the housing manager and said that I needed housing for my daughter and myself. The man pulled a standard sheet of paper out of his desk with a single-spaced list of names typed on it, of married couples coming to college that fall looking for off-campus housing. The housing manager also mentioned that the seminary across the street from the college had a similar waiting list. He said he was sorry, but nothing was or would be available for the fall semester. Frank and I walked to the door, filled with disappointment.

Frank was just opening the door to leave when the phone rang. Frank and the housing manager had not finished their good-byes, so he motioned for us to stay for a moment. After he got off the phone, he smiled and said that he had just talked with a young widow who had two daughters. She had come down to school and was now getting married.

He said, "Why don't we keep her apartment for you young widows who come down here to find a husband?" In response, I said that I was absolutely not coming to school to find a husband. He smiled and said, "You can have her apartment." In a matter of forty-five minutes, I had been accepted into college without a transcript and had a place for Teri and me to live.

On the way back to Ohio, I still was not sure what God was saying because I was so new to learning how to receive direction, and to know if the direction is really from Him. I shared with Frank the uncertainty that I was feeling and he shared some thoughts with me. He said that if I was driving down the highway and was coming upon a very sharp curve, would the sign for the curve be five miles ahead or just in front of where it actually was located? I replied that it would be right where the curve was, and Frank said that God would give me direction at the correct time.

When I arrived home, Mom came out to meet me on the front porch. To my surprise, she told me that my dad had been transferred to Maryland and that I would either have to move with them or find another place to live. For the next two weeks, I looked at homes to buy, but there was no peace in my heart. A home would look good on the listings and would seem fine from the outside, but when I would walk inside I would feel no peace or excitement at all. I couldn't picture Teri and myself living in any of those houses.

I finally decided that God was telling me to move to Kentucky and attend Asbury College that fall. Because I had married right after high school, had only lived thirty minutes from my parents, and had lived with them since Galen's death, moving was a big step for me. Mom drove down with Teri and me and helped us get settled in the two-bedroom duplex apartment that I had rented. She told me later that she cried all the way home after leaving us there by ourselves, knowing that we didn't know anyone, and would be lonely.

The most amazing thing happened! From the time I arrived in Wilmore, I never experienced any loneliness. Jesus was so close to me that my little apartment seemed to be filled with His presence.

The first night Teri and I were by ourselves, I was a little scared when I went to bed. As I prayed, I asked the Lord to put an angel on each corner of the roof of my apartment and to put an angel with a flaming sword at each window and door. After praying, I felt very safe and secure as I went to sleep.

A Love Fulfilled

By October 1966, I had been living in Wilmore for about three months. Grace, one of the women from the seminary, told me that she would like me to meet a certain seminary student. His name was Jim Parker, he was a man who loved the Lord, and she really respected him. She arranged for us to meet the next day in her dorm lounge.

I was so nervous when I went to meet Jim. I felt completely unprepared, both in my heart and in my appearance. I had washed my long dark brown hair and it hadn't gotten dry enough by the time I had to leave to arrive there on time. Besides that, I didn't know what to wear. I had been a housewife, not a college student. I had gone shopping before moving to Kentucky to go to college, and bought several suits with heels to match, which were not what college girls were wearing. I finally picked out a red and white double knit cotton dress that was pretty simple and off I went.

I was a bundle of nerves driving over to the dorm where I was to meet Grace and Jim. What would he be like? I made some wrong choices during my "dark night of the soul" while living in Newark, and I didn't want to repeat them. Was I in a place to put what God wanted for my life first and foremost? During the time that I lived in Newark, I had dated several men. There were specific qualities that I admired about each one, but when I prayed and told the Lord that if they were not the one for me to close the door, the relationship pretty much ended immediately. Was I willing for this to happen again?

When I walked into the dorm, I saw him immediately. Who was this man looking at me from across the room? He appeared to be around five feet nine inches tall, with thick, wavy, sandy brown hair. He reminded me of my favorite movie star, William Holden, who starred in "Love Is A Many-Splendored Thing. " Jim was the same height and body build as William Holden. As I looked into his clear blue eyes, I instantly saw warmth and acceptance, and my nervousness evaporated. We had an amazing time talking, and he asked me to go out for dinner with him the next week. .

I was so excited to be going on a date with Jim that I didn't eat much for breakfast or lunch that day. Jim picked me up in a borrowed car that several of the seminary students used. We were both at ease as we drove the twenty minutes to the small café that Jim had chosen. The waitress brought our menus and Jim asked me what I would like to have to eat.

I said, "What are you having?"

He said, "Just a piece of pie and coffee."

I knew that I should take my lead from what he was going to order, so I ordered just pie and coffee, although I was hungry enough to eat everything on the menu.

I found out later, after Jim and I were married, that he only had enough money for me to eat that night. Jim worked three jobs to put himself through Bible school. He was only eating two sparse meals a day to have enough money to get through seminary. Jim's determination to follow God's calling was one of the many qualities that endeared him to me.

Two weeks later, Teri and I went to a program at her preschool. The teacher made a few announcements and then said, "Why don't all the fathers take their children to see their work, while the mothers fix the cookies and punch?" I suddenly realized that

Teri was the only child without a father. I was trying to figure out what to do next when Jim appeared from the back of the room. He took Teri by the hand and led her to the area where the other children and their fathers were going.

My heart melted at the sight of Jim taking Teri by the hand; this was the first time that I saw what was really in Jim's heart. I saw his compassion, and I was amazed at what I saw. In the past, the men I dated weren't very interested in Teri. To them she was simply a hindrance to their relationship with me, but Jim was different. I was totally impressed with Jim and how he cared for Teri.

Jim and I would spend hours talking about our relationships with the Lord, and I really fell in love with Jim spiritually before I did emotionally and physically. After we had dated for several weeks, Jim felt that I needed to date other men since I didn't have any other experience dating dedicated Christian men. Jim didn't want me to think that I was in love with him because of his Christian testimony, rather than him as a person. Jim didn't want me to mix up admiring him for being in love with him. He wanted a wife who was in love with him, but also loved him for who he was.

One afternoon, a seminary student named Ron asked me to go to the seminary cafeteria for pie. As we walked into the cafeteria, I noticed Jim eating a bowl of soup. We hadn't been there more than a few moments when Jim got up and left with his food uneaten. Ron and I ate our pie and talked a little while. When we started up the stairs to leave, guess who was coming down the steps as we were going up? You guessed it: Jim. He looked at us, and he was an odd shade of green, which I maintain to this day. After that incident, Jim decided that I didn't need to date around anymore. Jim and I were married four months later. That was forty-seven years ago!

We decided to get married in a small church in the older section of Wilmore. We wanted to be married in the small seminary chapel where we would pray together, but it ended up being too small for the number of people invited to the wedding. We wanted a very small, plain wedding since I had a large wedding with my first marriage. I told Jim I only wanted a solid gold band for a wedding ring. Although I had lots of money in the bank, Jim insisted on paying for the wedding. He had only $100 for us to spend. My Mom and Dad bought the cake and punch.

I bought a tan lace dress and a little pillbox hat with netting that came out of the top. After we bought everything we needed, I realized that I only had $1.50 left for flowers. I went to a small florist and asked how much three long-stemmed roses would cost. The florist said $.50 each. All I wanted was three roses to symbolize the Trinity. The woman asked me if I wanted the roses in little vials of water. She said that vials would cost an extra $.50. So I said no and left the florist. The next morning, on the day of the wedding, I checked my roses in the refrigerator and discovered that they were wilted. While I was walking down the aisle, I had to hold my hand beneath the top of the roses so they wouldn't droop.

The funny thing is that none of this mattered to me. What mattered was that God had been faithful to give me a man who loved the Lord and who loved Teri and me, and who I loved.

The Bridal Suite

I didn't know until months later that Jim actually didn't have any money for our honeymoon until people at the reception gave him some cash. No one but Jim knew that he didn't have any money—he had just held the need up to the Lord in prayer. Jim was determined not to use any of my money, and he never did. He told me to pack for warm weather, but he kept where we were going a surprise.

God was so gracious to us on our honeymoon, starting with where we spent our wedding night. Jim had reserved a room at a mid-priced motel. After the wedding, we took the leftover cake and punch to Kentucky Village. Kentucky Village was a juvenile delinquent facility where Jim had been a volunteer for two years, working with delinquent teenagers convicted of any sort of felony charges. He taught Bible classes to the teens.

When we finally arrived at the motel, we found out that they didn't have a room for us and that nothing else was available in town because Lexington was hosting the basketball playoffs. Jim was very discouraged and sick at heart. We didn't know what to do, so we drove down the road to the big Holiday Inn. When Jim went in to ask if they had a room, the clerk said that they were all sold out. As Jim was leaving, the clerk mentioned that he did have one room unoccupied but that he was sure Jim would not want it because the only unoccupied room in the entire

110-room motel was the bridal suite. We stayed in the beautiful bridal suite for our wedding night with white satin sheets and a circular bed. We never would have spent the money for such a beautiful room, but God had other ideas.

The next day, we continued driving to southern Kentucky. We spent five days at a brand new resort that was built to resemble a Swiss chalet. When we walked into the lobby, Jim and I were about the third couple in line. We listened as the clerk registered the other guests and heard the prices they were paying for their rooms. When we were next in line and Jim asked for a room, the man quoted us a rate half of what the other people were being charged. We felt like it was God's intervention in our behalf because we had never seen the people in the resort before and we didn't appear different from any one else in the line. The people in line behind us were charged the same amount as the people in line in front of us—double what we were charged. After our time at the resort, we continued our trip to New Orleans and continued to have a wonderful honeymoon.

Off The High Dive

I must add a particular story here to describe an important lesson I learned. I don't know if you can tell from anything you have read in this book so far, but I am not and never have been a shy person. I always have been willing to live on the edge. When I was younger, I didn't have the common sense not to push Jim into a swimming pool.

Jim and I had just finished having a very romantic dinner at the resort, where we spent five nights during our honeymoon. I remember that I wore a powder blue linen suit and Jim wore his blue wool suit. After dining, we stopped by the swimming pool to play a game of ping-pong. While we were playing, the ping-pong ball fell into the water, and Jim had to walk on a small ledge between the shallow pool and the deeper pool to retrieve it. When he bent over to pick up the ball, I couldn't help but run over and push him into the water.

As his head broke the surface of the water, I thought, "What have you done?"

I saw the look on his face and took off running down the hallway to the hotel lobby, thinking that he wouldn't do anything to me in front of a group of people. Boy, was I wrong! I could hear the slosh-slosh-slosh of Jim behind me running towards me with shoes full of water.

When Jim caught up with me, he threw me over his shoulder in one full sweep of his arm. Back down the hallway we went, toward the pool. I could not have imagined what Jim was going to do to me, but I didn't have much time to wonder, as he started climbing the ladder on the high diving board.

As we neared the top, I realized Jim was going to throw me into the pool, so I quickly threw off the hairpiece I had on the top of my French-twist styled hair to keep it from getting wet. People were standing around in wide-eyed amazement as my hairpiece went flying down to the concrete pool edge, and I was thrown off of the high dive in my beautiful blue suit and high heels. I must have been quite a sight flying through the air. That was the first and last time in forty-seven years I have ever pushed Jim into a swimming pool with all of his clothes on.

Apart from the dip in the pool, Jim and I had a wonderful, relaxed honeymoon full of loving one another, caring for one another, and sharing our lives together as husband and wife. When we returned home, Jim, Teri, and I all went back to school during the week and spent the weekends ministering in Lexington.

Chapter Four

SEASON OF VISION
FULFILLED

Isaiah 58:6, "Is not this the kind of fasting I
have chosen:...Is it not to share your food
with the hungry and to provide the poor wanderer with shelter — when you see the naked,
to clothe him, and not to turn away from your
own flesh and blood?"

Switchblades and a Story To Tell

had only been in Wilmore about a month when
Teri's daycare provider told me that her sister
and husband, who had a small mission in the inner
city of Lexington, needed someone to help with the
children's ministry. She arranged for me to meet the
couple and I agreed to help them. Previously, I had
always lived in small towns and had no experience

with a town the size of Lexington, Kentucky, which had a population of about 100,000 in 1967.

In Lexington, there was a very depressed area called Davis Bottoms, and one next to it called Irish Town. The two neighborhoods were about one-half mile from the heart of town. I decided to visit the areas on Saturday afternoon with my college girlfriend, Sheri. I didn't know what to wear because I had never been in a poverty environment. Finally, I decided on a green and white dress that I would wear each time visiting the area. Over the next year, I became known as the woman in the green and white dress.

When Sheri and I went into the poor area of town the first Saturday, I took my only Bible, a large black Thompson Chain King James version I had gotten for college. I took off my diamond rings because I didn't want the people to be embarrassed at what they didn't have. (At least, that was my thinking at the time.)

Sheri and I parked my car at the mission and decided to walk different directions to meet people. Afterwards, we realized how naïve we were. I had only walked about two blocks when a group of black men in their twenties surrounded me. I didn't feel afraid until I saw the people on their porches all go into their homes so that I was the only one in sight besides the men surrounding me. One of the young men opened a switchblade knife and held it to my throat.

Another man said, "What are you doing here?"

At this, I gulped and said that I had come to tell people about Jesus and that He loved them. I went on to tell them how Jesus had changed my life and told them some of the things God had done for me. One young man who stood beside me told the man who was holding the switchblade to my throat to let me go.

He said, "You are for real, aren't you?"

I said, "Yes," and continued to tell them that Jesus loved them the same way that He loved me.

I told them the story of how I had smoked two packs of Camels or Lucky Strikes a day. My father-in-law (the one like Boss Hog) had offered me $500 to quit and I said no. After I had become a Christian, I continued to smoke. About a year later, I was playing cards with a neighbor lady and watching a Billy Graham crusade on television. As we watched the TV, Billy Graham was talking about our bodies being the temple of the Holy Spirit. I sat there and became very uncomfortable as I thought about smoking. The girl who was playing cards with me didn't have any idea what was going on inside of me. As I sat there, I had a vision of myself as a large gold Buddha with smoke coming out my ears and nose.

At that moment, I told the Lord that I had never been willing to quit smoking (except when I made the deal with Him to get pregnant), but that I was willing to be willing to be willing to be willing, and so on. I think I was about six "willings" away from being willing. I told God that if He would take my willing to be willing, I would give smoking to Him because I wanted my life to please Him and didn't want anything to be an idol in my life. I put out the cigarette that I was smoking. The next morning when I got up, I realized I didn't want a cigarette. My normal morning routine, at that time in my life, was to have a cup of coffee and a cigarette for breakfast.

People asked me why I wasn't smoking. I didn't know how to tell them what had happened to me, so I said I had a sore throat. After several months, I finally had the courage to tell whoever asked me that Jesus had actually taken away my desire to smoke when I committed it to Him. That was the last cigarette I ever smoked. I realized that all God needed was my willingness and He would do the rest

When I was done telling the story of how I quit smoking cigarettes, I told the young men surrounding me on the street that Jesus cared about our lives and was there to help us when we turned to Him. I went on to tell them that Jesus had died on the cross for their sins and that He loved them. We talked for a while, then we said our good-byes, and I went on my way.

Dirty Faces and Hungry Hearts

Jim and I spent most Saturdays and Sundays in the depressed area of Lexington called Davis Bottoms. We would spend Saturdays visiting the children in their homes and walking around the neighborhoods, talking with people as they congregated outdoors. The homes were very small and overcrowded and were always very hot, as no one had air conditioning or fans. Many times, I would carry a puppet for the children to see and invite them to a puppet show. We called these weekend meetings "Junior Church," since it was for the children.

Eventually, about twenty Asbury College students went to the Bottoms with us on Sunday afternoons. We walked the streets, picked up the children and walked with them to the mission. We all looked like

Pied Pipers because each college student was walking with about fifteen to twenty children. We usually had about one hundred to one hundred and fifty children at our Bible classes.

One Saturday afternoon while visiting the area, I came upon a long brick building on a side street. The building resembled a motel with eight units. As I knocked on the first door, I realized that each small room housed a family. A woman came to the door with a white sheet wrapped around her, fastened with a large safety pin at her shoulder. She invited me in.

As I stepped through the door, I was not mentally prepared for what I encountered. Two small crippled children lay on beds. Each bed was the size of a cot. The metal bed frames had four legs but were smaller than a normal twin-sized bed. None of the beds had any type of mattresses, pads, or bedding to protect the children's tender skin from the pain and irritation of lying on iron mesh screening. Their skin looked wet as if covered with what looked like slime, but was in fact a mixture of sweat and dirt.

Since the children on the beds weren't wearing any clothing or diapers, their excrements fell onto the floor under their beds. It was so hot in the room that I felt like I was in a sauna.

The place had such a horrible stench that I started having dry heaves. I had to excuse myself to go outside for a moment to get some fresh air and to ask the Lord to help me cope with the smell.

A total of six children lived in this one room with their mother and father. Besides the two crippled children on the iron beds, I noticed two other children playing on the floor as well as two school-aged children.

I made arrangements to pick up the two school-aged children the next day for the puppet show at the mission.

On Sunday, I went to pick up the little girl named Janice, who was seven years old, and the little boy named Randy, who was about five years old. They were both delighted to come with me. While we were walking to the mission, hand in hand, Randy looked up at me with a pitiful look on his face and said that his face was dirty because his mommy didn't have time to wash it. I remember telling him that he looked just fine to me, and he beamed with joy as he squeezed my hand.

That day, we gave Janice and Randy a picture of Jesus I had gotten from a church that gave us leftover Sunday school material. Every Sunday following that day, when I went to pick up the children, I would see the picture stuck to the wall with chewing gum.

Several years later, when we were living at Christ Center, the welfare department called and told us that they had found two children by the name of Janice and Randy in a home without food and necessities. The welfare department wanted to take the children into custody, but the children said they would not go unless someone called Jim and Dixie.

Janice and Randy told the social workers that they were waiting for us to pick them up to take them to the mission to tell them more about Jesus and His love for them.

When the social workers found Janice and Randy, they had been in their home by themselves without electricity, food, or heat for three days. By this time, they had moved from the one-room apartment into a house several blocks from the first location where I had first visited their family. Their father had been put in jail, and their mother had left them. At this time, they were about nine and seven years old.

Janice and Randy lived with us at Christ Center for six weeks until the social workers insisted on putting them back with their parents, who had been found. When the children came to us, we were told that Randy was retarded because he couldn't read or write.

I started going over his numbers and alphabet with him every night, and within a couple of weeks he was doing well with both. He wasn't retarded or even a slow learner, but no one had taken an interest in him or taken the time to teach him.

Janice and Randy had never worn underwear before living with us. We even taught the children how to brush their teeth. The two children warned us not to leave the cereal on the kitchen table at night, or the rats would eat it all.

When the social workers came to pick up the children, Randy didn't want to leave with them. It broke my heart when the social worker picked up Randy and carried him away, screaming and kicking. I will never forget the look on little Randy's face as his hands tried to grab hold of me when they carried him away. The next day, we went to visit their parents to offer any help that we could, but they had left during the night. We never saw the children again, but the memory of them is embedded in my heart and mind.

Chipped Cups and Cracked Plates

Before Christ Center started, and while we were still living in Wilmore, a family in Irish Town invited Jim, Teri, and me to come over for dinner.

When we arrived at their small home made of concrete blocks, the family was nothing but smiles. We found out that we were their first guests ever. The table was set with chipped and cracked dishes. Most of the cups were missing handles, and we were given various types of eating utensils. Our hosts told us later that they had to borrow dishes to have enough for us all to eat on.

Jim and I had talked to Teri before we arrived and told her to eat what she could and to take very small bites so that our hosts wouldn't be offended that we didn't eat whatever they served us. She was a real trooper and behaved well. I was the one who had difficulty eating; I was in the first months of my pregnancy and was very sensitive to smells and tastes.

For dinner, the family served us two kinds of meat and five desserts. They told us that since they had never had guests, they didn't know what type of food to serve. They asked a neighbor who told them to have lots of meat and dessert when they had company. I doubt if their neighbors were speaking from experience.

The family served us chicken and dumplings with chicken fat floating all over the top of the bowl. The dumplings were so greasy I could hardly get my stomach to accept each bite. They also served us very tough roast beef.

Next came the desserts. As we ate the raw cookie dough and partially cooked cake, served with such warm smiles, we kept thanking them for inviting us.

The parents could not read or write, so they couldn't read the baking directions on the package of the cookie dough. They told us they just had to guess at how long to bake the cake. They had only added water to the cake mix because they couldn't read the directions to determine what ingredients to add.

When we left, our hosts were delighted because Jim had eaten three plates of the chicken and dumplings and some of everything else. To this day, I think Jim has a cast iron stomach, and I know he has a lot of love for people.

My lesson that evening was that only God's love does not pull back from the unlovely. I was very quickly made aware that only God loves the unlovely and that I can only be a reflector of His love. God does not expect me to have the capacity to love unselfishly, and He doesn't want me to place my confidence in my own abilities, but He wants me to be dependent on Him and on His abilities to work through my life.

Shoes for Lilly

After having the Junior Church at the mission for the children who lived in Irish Town and Davis Bottoms, we knew the living situation of a lot of the children. As time for school approached in August, Jim and I talked about the fact that the children needed help with buying shoes and clothing. We decided on a plan of action to help with the situation. We got together about $300 that we could spend. In today's ecomony, this amount doesn't sound like much money, but in the late 1960s, $5 could buy a pair of children's shoes or a set of clothes. We bought the boys and girls shoes as a first priority, but, if the children already had shoes, we bought the boys a shirt and the girls a dress. We bought clothes made out of either all polyester or half-cotton and half-polyester, so that they could be washed and hung up to dry. We thought that if the children had to take care of their own laundry, this was the best option because nothing needed to be ironed.

I spent most Saturdays visiting the homes of the children and just being a presence in the area, talking to the people. As I went down one of the streets one day, I noticed Lily playing outside without any shoes and with a very bad runny nose. We saw Lily every week when she came to Junior Church. She had long blond hair and beautiful blue eyes and was six years old and in the first grade of school. It was late October and the temperature had already turned cold. My first thought was that her alcoholic father had sold her shoes, so I knocked on the door to find out why she was barefoot in the cold weather. Her mother, who was a very sweet woman, answered the door. After saying hello, I asked her why Lily wasn't wearing the shoes we had bought her because it was so cold outside. She took me inside her home and showed me Lily's shoes that were wrapped in a piece of cloth, lying on a shelf in the living room. Lily's mom told me that Lily was so proud of her shoes that, as soon as she arrived home from school, she wrapped them in the cloth and put them on the shelf so that they would not get dirty.

Grandma Hall

Grandma Hall was straight from a page in a book about the life of a pioneer woman. She still made her own lye soap from ashes and other ingredients. Her house didn't have any electriity, so she used kerosene lamps and cooked on a wood-burning stove. Because she lived in an area that was in the heart of Lexington but was unincorporated, the city was not required to provide city services.

The first time I met the lady we always called Grandma Hall, I was visiting the homes on her street, talking to the people about Junior Church for the children and asking if anyone was interested in having a Bible study. She invited me in to her home, and as I talked to her and her husband about the Lord and how much He love them, her husband dropped to his knees weeping. He told me how he had murdered a man some thirty years before and wanted to repent and ask Jesus to forgive him. When he got up from the floor, his face had a calm and peaceful look on it that had not been there previously.

We visited Grandma Hall and her husband for several years until she died.

Christmas Gifts for the Children

Every Christmas season that we were having Junior Church at the mission, we would buy and collect toys for the children. Jim would borrow a pickup truck, load the wrapped gifts in the back, and head to Davis Bottoms and Irish Town to pass out the gifts on Christmas Eve. These were the only gifts that many of the children would receive for Christmas.

One memory that I will never forget involves a little kitchen set that was donated to us for a child. It stood about four feet tall and had a stove, refrigerator, and sink all hooked together. When Jim was delivering it to the family he had chosen, as he drove up in front of the house and the children saw the kitchen set in the back of the pickup truck, one of the little girls got so excited, her body started shaking. It was the only gift that the family received that Christmas.

Availability, Not Ability

You are probably wondering about the place called Christ Center that I have mentioned several times. Christ Center was a wonderful testimony of how awesome God is and how He uses the foolish things of the world to confound the wise. God chose to use college students when He raised up Christ Center, instead of trained, experienced people who had done that kind of work before. I think that He used us so that people would see that He was the one who did it, since it was apparent that it was not us.

While I was attending Asbury College, Jim and I worked with fifteen to twenty college students, ministering to the people in the areas I have mentioned in Lexington. During the winter of 1967, two teenage girls hitchhiked twenty miles, in very cold weather, without coats or warm clothes, from Lexington to our home in Wilmore for help. They were having trouble and didn't know where to turn but to us. At the time, I was leading a Bible study for about ten teenage girls from Davis Bottoms who had become Christians through our nighttime street meetings.

During the summer of 1967, we had street meetings every Friday night in the areas known as Davis Bottoms and Irish Town. One of the men from Asbury

College, Gil, who had worked for a ministry the year before in the ghettoes of New York City, led a singing team for us. A group of us, all college students, would load up a VW van with instruments and drive into Lexington. The singing team would play instruments and sing and draw a crowd. Then Jim would preach and share the gospel. After Jim spoke, we all would go into the crowd and pray for people.

After working in the inner city area with the children for about two years, and seeing the need to be close by to help them, we started praying with another couple every day at 5 p.m. in the seminary chapel for God to raise up a youth center in Lexington.

One afternoon when I was alone in our duplex, I heard a knock at our front door. It was a door that no one ever used, and anyone who knew us from the college would have come to the back door that opened onto the driveway.

I thought it was strange when I answered the door and found a woman standing there. She introduced herself as Beverly Fortune. She said she was a reporter for the *Lexington Herald*, the town newspaper. She had heard of our work in the inner city and asked if she could interview me.

The following Sunday, the story of what we had been doing at the mission with the children and our dream of having a youth center for the teens was on the front page of the Lexington newspaper. It has always amazed me how this happened, because we were busy in the ministry and would never have contacted a newspaper.

We had been praying for God to provide a building for us in the inner city area as a local facility to help the people. We found an old building that was used for a school in the early 1900s and had been a warehouse for many years. The building had been vacant for about fifteen years and was in total disrepair, but we talked the owner into renting it to us. As collateral for the building, Jim and I actually offered all the savings we had left from my money. The owner was pretty dubious about our renting the building without the guarantee of our money in an escrow account for him.

While all this was happening, I was about seven months pregnant with our first child. Jim was in his last year of schooling at Asbury Seminary, and I was finishing up my second year of college. I took off the last quarter of college because I was expecting to deliver our baby soon.

Because of the article in the Lexington newspaper, Jim and I were asked to come and share our story at Christ Church, a large Episcopal church in downtown Lexington. Christ Church had a regular Wednesday evening dinner and sharing time.

After our sharing on Wednesday evening, the rector of Christ Church asked me if I would speak at his church service the following Sunday. I accepted, but was extremely fearful because he told me that I only had twenty minutes to speak and that I could not speak any longer than my allotted time.

I looked so funny when I got up to speak because I was very, very pregnant. I was so pregnant that the microphone was a couple of feet from my mouth.

I could not stand in front of the microphone, so they had to set the microphone beside me. I was nervous while speaking, but when I finished, I had talked for almost exactly twenty minutes. I didn't have any notes, but I just spoke from my heart. The only reason I could do it was because I knew God was in total control and not my oratory abilities.

During my talk, I shared the burden we had for a youth center in Lexington and the work we were doing in Davis Bottoms and Irish Town. I ended with the story of the newborn baby in the cardboard box with a diarrhea-stained blanket and roaches. I told the audience that this poor area was underneath and beside a busy viaduct. Most people did not even know of the conditions that existed in the poor area of town that they drove over daily on their way to work or shopping.

After leaving the church service, a young girl said to her father, "Daddy, she doesn't mean our town, does she?"

Her father replied that I did mean their town, but that he would do something about it.

Later that week, that man called to see if I could meet him and some other men at his factory and tell them my story. When I arrived at his factory, there were about ten men around a conference table. I shared the burden God had given us.

Since Jim was finishing his studies in seminary and couldn't go with me, I asked another person, Paul, to come with me for support.

After the meeting, a man named Al from the conference asked me to go to lunch with him at the

Campbell House, which was one of Lexington's nicest hotels at that time, to meet a friend of his. Paul and I got in his car and drove to the Campbell House, where we sat down in the dining room with Al and his friend Art, who owned the Campbell House. Al asked me to share my story, so I told Art about my burden and my testimony. The more I talked about Jesus, the more nervous Art seemed to be. After I was done talking, Art asked, "Dixie, do you need some furniture?"

Al said that anything like a couch would be great.

At this, Art said, "I have one hundred rooms of furniture sitting in two warehouses. I was going to ship them to Florida, but you can have them for your youth center." Included in this furniture were one hundred bedroom sets complete with mattresses, curtains, beautiful wool carpets, about eight couches, and dining room tables and chairs. I remember I was so excited and talked so fast when I got home that it took Jim a while to understand what I was saying.

The offer of free furniture happened in April 1968. At that time, Jim and a group of people were working on the building most nights, patching walls and doing other repairs. Fixing the building seemed like an endless job that would never get finished.

Moving Day

Two weeks later, the owner of the Campbell House called and said that the furniture needed to be moved out of the warehouses by the following Saturday. It was Thursday when he called us. We didn't know where to turn for help, so I called Mary B., a wonderful

Christian lady who had helped us so much in the ministry in the Bottoms.

The winter before, we had rented a small duplex in Davis Bottoms. A friend of Jim's from seminary, named Hino, moved into the house to be closer to the needy people. A friend named Mary, who paid house cleaners to clean her home, went down to Davis Bottoms with me to clean this concrete block duplex. To say that it was dirty was an understatement, but I will never forget the afternoon that Mary and I cleaned this place. Mary was right in the thick of it with me, with rubber gloves up to our elbows in the dirty bathroom.

I called Mary to see if we could borrow her pickup truck for the day to move the furniture. She asked me what I needed it for. When I told her, she said she would call me back.

In about an hour, Mary called me and said that a friend of hers was a plumbing contractor. She had called him, and he told her that this next Saturday was the only day of the year that he didn't need his two large trucks because they were taking inventory. He gave us the use of the trucks and the drivers for the day. God had the situation in His hands and showed us once again that He was in control of what we were doing.

Students who had been working with us in Davis Bottoms helped us move all the furniture and carpets into the building we had leased.

Jim had the carpets laid flat on the floor of what had once been the gymnasium when the building was a school. We had so many carpets that the pile almost reached the ceiling.

We moved furniture all day, and then realized that we could not leave all the furniture in an old building in the inner city without someone there to watch over it. Jim and I decided that we would have to move in right away, so we did. It is amazing to me now to think that we moved into that building with me a month away from delivering our baby, and with a six year-old child, but that is exactly what we did.

Restoring A Messy Building

The building was an absolute mess. None of the bathrooms worked, and there were no cooking facilities. I had an electric roaster oven that I used to cook our meals, then I would clean it out and put warm water in it to wash Teri at night before she went to bed.

We put our furniture in an annex on one side of the large building. We made a living room and two bedrooms for us to live in. I strung curtains on rope in our living quarters to try to make our new home more normal in a very abnormal environment.

Jim and I woke up the first morning we lived at the center with a hippie girl, Susan, watching us sleep. I still don't know how she got into the building. She ended up staying with us for several months. I will never forget one instance when Teri was home sick from school. Susan fixed Teri lunch and Teri complained to me that she didn't want to eat the soup because it didn't taste good. I found out that Susan had made the soup out of all the leftover salad from dinner the night before.

After a couple of weeks of trying to get the building in shape by human effort, we got on our knees in front of our old couch and said, "Jesus, we can't do this anymore. We have tried and it's more than we can do. It is Your center, so we are giving it back to You to fix up."

Besides my being ready to have a baby, Jim was finishing up his last year at Asbury seminary and was graduating in two weeks. The next morning, Jim and Teri left for school. Teri was still attending school in Wilmore, so Jim dropped her off on his way to the seminary, just a short distance from Teri's school.

I was walking around the building, trying to decide what to do, when I heard the doorbell at the side door. It was about 10:00 in the morning. I went to the door and a white-haired man named Jerry introduced himself. He told me that he had always tithed his money to the Lord, but God had told him to tithe his time and he had come to us to volunteer his services. I asked him what he did, and he told me that he was a carpet installer. I happily invited him in and showed him the room full of carpets piled to the ceiling.

Jerry started laying the carpet that day. He told me later that he had told the Lord that he would lay carpet for us until he got work. He did not get any calls for work for three weeks, until the majority of the carpet was laid. I am sure Jerry got an extra crown to lay at Jesus' feet for all the work he did for us. He also provided all the installation materials free of charge.

At noon on the same day, I heard another knock at the side door. When I opened the door, a man named Ed introduced himself. Ed said that he had heard that we needed some plumbing done and he was a plumbing contractor. I showed Ed around, told him the vision God had given us for a youth center, and showed him our bathrooms. There were two bathrooms in the building, but the toilets had been filled with sand. Ed came back with a crew that day and started putting in showers, toilets, and plumbing for our washer and hot water heaters. Amazingly, Ed did not charge us a penny for his work, including the supplies.

At five o'clock that afternoon, there was a knock at the front door. Five men in blue jeans and work shirts, with leather pouches around their waists and coils of copper wire over their shoulders, appeared before me. They told me that they were electricians from the University of Kentucky and that they had heard we needed some electrical work done. They worked until midnight, putting in 220-volt circuits and fixing all the electrical circuits that we needed.

I spoke at a Kiwanis luncheon in Lexington during the first year that Christ Center started and told the men the story of Christ Center. I challenged them to build a house and in one day have the carpet-layer, plumber and electrician all come and do the work and not charge anything. They thought such an idea was impossible, but God did it for His ministry!

Jim felt very strongly that the Christ Center ministry should be run in the same way that George Mueller ran his orphanages in England many years ago. George Mueller didn't let his needs be known to anyone except to God, in prayer. We decided that we would not let anyone know our needs except the Lord, in prayer, and agreed that this would be the sign that God wanted us to continue in this ministry.

The first summer, I kept the books and witnessed first hand the miraculous provision of the Lord. At the end of each month, I would add up the money we needed to pay the bills and the money that was given to us. Many times it came out to within $2. I still have the small ledger in which I kept the bookkeeping records. One month we took in $1,098.75 and needed $1,097 for bills. Neither the staff nor we received any salary, so we also had to pray for sufficient money for our own needs.

In retrospect, we should have tried to provide salaries for the staff who were college students and gave up their summer jobs to work at the Center without any pay. Most of them trusted God to bring in what they needed for their next year's tuition and other necessities.

We are forever indebted and thankful for the students who gave their time and talents to work with the inner-city children during that period. They did it purely out of their love for the children and their dedication to the Lord. The Lord also brought some married couples to live at the Center and to be a part of the ministry.

God's Turf

Christ Center was located on the corner of Mill Street and Maxwell Street, three streets from the main part of town. We eventually painted the building a light shade of green with darker green trim. As we walked into the building through a large wooden door with arched overhead windows, a ninety-four-foot-long by eight-foot-wide hallway welcomed us.

Draperies that had been taken down from the entrance of the Campbell House perfectly fit the high windows over the doorway into the center. We painted the walls tan with green woodwork.

Entering the building, the first room on the right became our chapel. It was thirty-six feet wide by twenty-four feet. At one end of the chapel stood a twelve-foot-high, hand-made wooden cross made out of railroad ties . It was originally made for a sunrise Easter morning service held at the park across from the mission in Davis Bottoms. Many nights, the chapel would be filled with up to 100 teenagers and young adults seated Indian style on the carpet, singing worship songs accompanied by guitars. We eventually outgrew the downstairs chapel and moved into a much larger room on the second floor that was the size of the original gymnasium, which was seventy-two feet by thirty-six feet.

The room across from the original first floor chapel was made into bedrooms. Next to it were the men's bathrooms and showers. Proceeding down the hallway, the next room to the left was the dining room, which could seat the fifty to sixty people who lived at Christ Center. The lounge located across the hall from the dining room was large enough to fit six couches plus several occasional chairs. We arranged the furniture to provide several seating areas to make the spacious room more comfortable. The draperies were a perfect fit for the windows in the lounge. The couches were teal green and the draperies had been made to match the couches for the Campbell House Inn. Most of the rooms off the front hallway measured thirty-six feet by twenty-four feet.

The kitchen, next to the dining room, was an empty shell when we moved into the building, as were all the rooms. One of the college students, who was on staff and worked with us for the summer, told her father, who was a carpenter, that we didn't have any cabinets. He arrived at the Center with wood, hammers, nails, and all that was needed to turn the large room into a wonderful kitchen. He built two large twelve-foot-long islands full of cabinets. White formica tops were fashioned over the cabinets and a bar attached over the tops to hang the pots and pans. I picked a bright orange color to paint the cabinets, so the kitchen was bright and cheery as we walked into it. Meals were cooked in the kitchen to feed fifty to sixty people most nights, plus whoever else would wander in off the streets needing a hot meal.

Jim built six bedrooms at the end of the hallway in what once had been the gymnasium. I can remember one occasion when a man in a three-piece suit came into the center and asked to speak to the person in charge. I directed him to Jim, who was framing the wall for one of the bedrooms in the gymnasium. The man came back to me and said that the person in charge was not in the gym, but only a man in blue jeans on top of the wood beams, doing construction. I smiled as I told him that the person in blue jeans doing the work was indeed my husband, Jim.

Our living quarters were located in an annex that had been built on the right side of the school building. A hallway connected the former school building to the annex. Proceeding down the hallway to the right was a large dorm room that could sleep more than a dozen people. Proceeding down the hall, more bedrooms were on the right side, and turning to the left would be six more bedrooms. We put our living room furniture in the bedroom at the end of the hall, making it into a living room. Our bedroom opened off of the living room, and our children's bedroom opened off of ours. We arranged it this way so that no one could get into our children's bedroom without going through ours. The doors to the hallway from the bedrooms were permanently closed off, making them accessible only through the living room. We felt that this was an added protection for our children's safety.

A coffeehouse, called the Catacombs, was located in the basement of Christ Center under the annex. The stone walls were painted black, as they symbolized the dark time when the early Christians were martyred in the Coliseum in Rome. The Christians hid in the catacombs to escape being killed during the persecution.

The entertainment portrayed biblical answers to life as the staff performed musically and talked with the young people and college students who came from the University of Kentucky and the local high schools. Coffee, pizza, and soft drinks were served. The coffee house was open on the weekends.

The summer of 1968, we had several ministries going on in the afternoons. We had a new Volkswagen bus. Jim built a puppet stage that fit inside of it so that, when the side door was opened, the puppet stage fit into the opening. We drove into neighborhoods and the singing team, which consisted of several singers and guitar players, would start singing and a crowd would gather. After a few songs, some of us would put on a puppet show out of the side of the Volkswagen bus. After a time of prayer for the needs of the people, the new believers would be signed up to participate in a weekly Bible club in their neighborhood.

During the afternoon, we also had a Swap Shop on the second floor of the building. Families could bring whatever they had and swap it for clothing or furniture or what we had that they needed. I remember one time that a mother needed clothes for her children but didn't have anything to swap. She told us that she had two peach trees and that she would bring us peaches when her fruit trees bore their fruit. Several months later, the lady walked into the center bringing two large bags of fresh peaches. She had the clothes her children needed, plus her dignity.

A basketball hoop with a backdrop was fastened onto the large round fire escape attached to the side of the building. The fire escape resembled a large silo that we would expect to see on a farm, not in the heart of town. The fire escape had a circular slide inside that gave a thrill riding down, as long as elbows did not scrap on the sides. The blacktop parking lot was the scene of a continual afternoon game as the inner city guys gathered to play basketball. One of the boys spray-painted "God's Turf" on the backdrop to declare who owned the area.

Reflections

A season of vision fulfilled is a time that we can declare to the outside world that we have seen with our eyes that God answers prayer and that He is alive. Ecclesiastes 3:1 states, "There is a time for everything, and a season for every activity under heaven."

God gave us Isaiah 58:6-8 as our theme scripture when we were ministering at Christ Center.

"Is not this the kind of fasting I have chosen, to loose the chains of injustice and to untie the cords of the yoke, to set the oppressed free and break every yoke? Is it not to share your food with the hungry and to provide the poor wanderer with shelter — when you see the naked, to clothe him, and not to turn away from your own flesh and blood?"

God gives us opportunities to be His hands and His feet to the world around us. We need to have listening ears and willing hearts to respond when He calls us to serve others in His name. Lord, help us to be obedient to Your heart for the lost and hungry.

God, help us during our season of vision fulfilled to give You all of the glory and praise for what You have done. Help us to respond to You with a humble heart, for You are Almighty God, we are Your subjects.

Chapter Five

SEASON OF GOD'S PROVISION

Matthew 18:19-20, "Again, I tell you; that if two of you on earth agree about anything you ask for, it will be done for you by my Father in heaven. For where two or three come together in my name, there am I with them."

T-Bone Steaks Instead of Hot Dogs

A woman who heard me speak at Christ Church called to ask me if the staff of the Center would like to come to her country home for a barbecue the following Sunday afternoon at five o'clock. She told me she would provide everything but the meat. That week, I planned the menu so that we would have hamburger and hotdogs left to take to the barbecue.

As it happened, Jim and the staff members who worked with the children's ministry at the mission brought a van loaded with children home for lunch after church. The children ate all of the hamburger and hot dogs that I had kept for the barbecue. I was so frustrated when I realized that we wouldn't have any meat to take to the woman's house—the only thing she had asked us to bring. It would be so embarrassing!

We went back to our living room, got on our knees again, and prayed to the Lord. He was our only resource. The so-called "blue laws" in Kentucky at the time kept all the grocery stores closed on Sundays. Even if God brought us money to buy meat, no stores were open where we could purchase something that day. I decided just to take a nap, because there was nothing I wanted to do but hide from the situation by escaping in sleep. We were supposed to be at the woman's home at five o'clock.

At about three in the afternoon, there was a knock at the side door. Someone else answered the door and called for me. As I approached the door, I saw a very tall, large man wearing an Army uniform. He asked me if he was at Christ Center and I replied that he was. He told me that he had some supplies for us. I was in total amazement as he went to his truck and came back to me carrying a box that contained twenty-five one-inch-thick T-bone steaks, plus bags containing 100 pounds of oatmeal and 100 pounds of pinto beans.

I asked him how he happened to bring these things to us, because I knew that he had brought God's answer to our prayers for meat for the barbecue. The soldier responded that he had been at National Guard Camp for two weeks. After they had packed up the leftovers and as he was driving out of camp, an officer of higher rank yelled at him to take the supplies to Christ Center at the corner of Mill and Maxwell Street in Lexington, Kentucky. He had been at a camp about two hours from Lexington and had driven and found us.

In direct answer to our prayers, God provided T-bone steaks for us, when I was only originally planning to have hot dogs and hamburgers. That was another lesson about God's graciousness that I learned along the way! I have often wondered if the person who gave the orders to take the supplies to Christ Center was an angel dressed like an officer. In any case, the two National Guard officers were agents of the Lord on our behalf.

Another time, we needed hamburger for spaghetti sauce that we were planning to have for dinner. We had just decided to have meatless spaghetti sauce when a woman walked into the Center with twenty-five pounds of hamburger and a very interesting story. Her name was Ellen, and she was a remarkable Christian with a heart for God.

As we sat together, Ellen told her story to me. She had been shopping at the grocery store when she went by the meat counter. She had an impression while she was standing in front of the meat counter that she should buy some hamburger for Christ Center. When she first had the impression, she ignored it and continued shopping because she had never had an experience like that before. Ellen told me that as she continued walking up and down the aisles of the store, she became more and more restless in her spirit.

Finally, she went back to the meat counter and, as she stood there, said, "Okay, Lord, if this is You telling me this, how much meat do You want me to buy for Christ Center?" She arrived at Christ Center with the hamburger just as dinner was being prepared. God was not only paying our bills, but He was literally providing our daily food.

At one point, there was a major financial crisis at the Center. We had some bills due without the money to pay them, so we knew something was wrong. Normally we had a daily staff meeting when we would pray together and talk about the activities planned for the day.

At the time of the crisis, Jim presented the situation in the staff meeting. We discussed whether God was telling us to close the Center, because we had told God we would know how long we were to be in operation by seeing Him provide our needs.

As the staff members began to pray, God started convicting hearts of bitterness, jealousy, anger, and various sins that had surfaced from our living and working together. With the amount of tireless work that we were all putting into the ministries at the Center, coupled with a lack of sleep, sparks were bound to fly.

At the Center, our days were very busy. During the summer, the day would start at six a.m. with our personal devotions. We would have breakfast at seven o'clock. After breakfast, everyone would do the daily assigned cleaning chores. Then we would have our staff meeting and lunch. In the afternoon, there would be the street puppet ministry and Bible clubs. After dinner, we all would go out and hold a street meeting. Then, we would come back to open the coffeehouse and stay there until around midnight and start again at six o'clock the next morning.

Needless to say, after weeks of this schedule, tempers started to flare. However, because we were "Christians in ministry," we felt we had to keep all of our feelings of anger and frustration inside to look good.

In truth we were all exhausted, but we felt that we needed to keep this schedule to please God because He was paying the bills. Truthfully, I think we all were so young in the Lord, we hadn't learned how to deal with our carnality (sinful nature) properly.

As we prayed and God started convicting us of sin, we began going to one another, confessing our sins, and asking for forgiveness. Then one person got a pan of water and we actually washed each other's feet. We ended the time in unity as God's love flowed freely among us once again. After our time of worship and prayer ended, Jim walked out into the hallway. Just then, the mailman came and handed Jim some letters. In one of the letters was a check for the exact amount of our bills, over $500. It was obvious that God wanted us to continue ministering at the Center.

Spaghetti Over The Head

Jim and I lived at Christ Center with our children for two years. Teri was six years old when we moved into the Center, and Cheryl was born after we had been at the Center for a month. Cheryl was nine months old when I became pregnant with Heather. It was quite a challenge living at Christ Center with a young child, a toddler, and expecting another child. It was very difficult living at Christ Center with three children.

We ate in the dining room with sixty people, including the staff members and all the people living with us. We had all types of people living with us. Some were young people from the hippie culture who had committed their lives to the Lord and moved in with us while they adjusted to being drug-free and rehabilitated. We also had homeless people and inner-city people who were out of work. We would take anyone in who had a legitimate need and was willing to work for a meal. There was always some type of job around the Center to be done.

At mealtime, Cheryl, who was a year-and-a-half old, would entertain everyone by dumping spaghetti over her head. When everyone laughed at her, she thought it was great fun. Cheryl had shoulder-length platinum blonde hair with bangs, big blue eyes and a sweet, angelic look about her. It was very difficult not to laugh at her when she did inappropriate actions during dinner. It was getting more and more difficult to teach Cheryl what was allowed and what was not. Finally, Jim made one of the bedrooms into a small dining room for our family to eat meals by ourselves.

Another difficulty we faced while living at the Center was using the toilets. When I was trying to potty train Cheryl, I had to run her down a hallway about forty-five feet long. Many times when I got her there, the toilets were all occupied. Life progressively became more and more difficult, living at the Center with three children.

A Home for Us

About this time, Jim and I went to Texas to visit another inner city ministry. While we were away, the attorney for the Center and a member of the board of directors of our nonprofit organization talked to the staff about giving us a house to live in with our children. The attorney's grandmother had died and left the house to his brother and him. While we were in Texas, the staff members and young adults who lived at the Center painted the house for us and moved us in.

The house was painted in a very interesting way because the young people lacked any experience with house painting. Nothing was color coordinated. The downstairs bathroom was painted purple, and the kitchen was painted bright yellow and dark navy blue. We loved the home and were grateful for the love that the young people showed us by all their hard work.

We rented the house very cheaply because Bill, the attorney for the Center, gave us his half free and we only had to pay his brother's half. The house had been built in 1907 and was absolutely wonderful. It had hardwood floors, large rooms, four fireplaces, and an enclosed sun porch across the back of the house with walls of windows. French doors opened from the sun porch into the dining room. The house also had a remodeled master bedroom suite. In front of the house was a wide boulevard planted with large oaks, with cars driving one way.

I mention these last two features because they show how God can answer our deepest desires without us even praying for them. A year before we moved into our new home, Jim and I were invited to dinner at the home of the rector of Christ Church. As we were leaving, we stopped beside our car and started talking. At that time, we had never considered not living at Christ Center. We had moved everything we owned into the Center and were committed to stay for the rest of our lives.

While Jim and I were talking and admiring the rector's neighborhood, I mentioned to Jim that, if we ever had a house again, I would love to live on a tree-lined boulevard like the one on which the rector and his wife lived. Jim mentioned that he would like to have a bathroom off the master bedroom. We both laughed at our thoughts and went home to the Center without talking or thinking of them again.

The first week in our new home, the Lord reminded us of our conversation as we realized that the house in which we were now living did in fact have a master bedroom with a bathroom, and was located on the only other street in Lexington with a tree-lined boulevard. We loved our years living in the house on Transylvania Park.

The kitchen in our new home was an old one without any kitchen cabinets. There was not any counter space in the kitchen, since it was without cabinets. I did not have any place but the kitchen table to prepare food. There was an old kitchen cabinet that dated to the 1920s, but it was pretty useless. There was a pantry on the back porch for dishes and food.

As you can tell from my description, the kitchen was very rustic and provided me with many challenges, as I was always cooking for many guests.

A man who had lived at Christ Center had become a carpenter and was remodeling a house at that time. He called Jim and told him that if he would help him take the old cabinets out of the house, we could have them. Jim did this and rebuilt them to fit our home.

Now I had new cabinets in the kitchen, but no countertop or sink. Jim told me to go to a store and pick out the color of countertop that I liked, and to then look at the remnant stock. I went with a friend and I picked out a yellow countertop. When we went into the back room of the shop where they put remnants and leftovers, we found a yellow Formica countertop that was a foot longer than we needed for our kitchen. I called Jim and he told me he could cut the countertop to fit the top of the cabinets. God provided us with the exact color countertop for a fraction of the normal cost.

Now I had cabinets in my kitchen and a countertop, but just a hole where the sink would be. I didn't have to wait long before God provided the money to get a new sink. I always loved this kitchen because I papered the walls with yellow flowered wallpaper, had yellow gingham ruffled curtains on windows that went almost to the floor, and had a yellow floor. Even on a gloomy rainy day, I still felt like the sun was shining outside.

Even in our new home on Transylvania Park, daily life was similar to our time in Christ Center. Our home was always full of people, and at different times, we had several people living with us. Often we had teen-agers, who needed and wanted our help, staying in our home. They mostly came from Irish town, Davis Bottoms and other poor areas. We seldom ate dinner alone as a family, so we had our special family time in the morning at the breakfast table.

At our new home, I had a weekly Bible study for a group of women who included some of the wives of our board of directors and their friends. We would hold the Bible study in my living room, and several women would sit on the couch. This couch really had a life of its own as it had been through two years at Christ Center with many people sitting on it. It had been bought in Mount. Vernon, Ohio, moved to Newark, Ohio, and used in my small duplex in Wilmore, before being used at Christ Center. It had more than the normal wear and tear, but it had survived. It looked fine on the outside, but when someone would sit on it, a spring would sometimes poke through.

To remedy the problem, I kept a pair of pliers under the couch, and whenever a spring poked through, I would just cut off the part sticking out. I didn't think much about it until one day when Jim mentioned that he had noticed that the cushions in our couch were starting to sag. I showed Jim the pliers and told him how I had fixed the problem of springs sticking through. He could not believe that I had done this! The funny part was that I hadn't seen anything wrong with the idea, until the cushions started to sag.

100 Quarts of Beans

During our time at Transylvania Park, Jim and I were privileged to see God provide for every need. Jim was still working at the Center. We traveled a lot on weekends, speaking in churches about the ministry at Christ Center and how God answers prayer. Every penny we got from the churches was given to Christ Center. Jim would not use any money from the donations we received to pay for the gas we needed to drive to the churches. Instead, we prayed for God to provide gas money as well as for our other needs.

I can remember only one time that we got down to just a few dollars. We were out of shampoo, toothpaste, and deodorant. Jim and I went to K-Mart and had to decide which two items to buy because we only had $2. We decided on deodorant and toothpaste. We thought we would use bar soap to wash our hair, if necessary.

After buying the two items, we had ten cents left and bought a candy bar. I remember laughing as we left the store eating our candy bar.

When we got home, the mail had arrived. In the mail was a letter from a man in Indiana with a check for twenty-five dollars that had been mailed the week before. God knew what our needs would be, before we did.

God provided for us in many miraculous ways. One day a woman from Gamier, Ohio, called to tell us that she had a side of beef for us. She proceeded to tell me her story. Her husband had bought her a calf for a birthday gift. It became ill and was dying, so she prayed for the calf to get better. She told the

Lord that if He would heal her calf, when it grew up and she butchered it, she would give half of the meat to us. After she prayed, the calf got up as if nothing was wrong with it.

I can remember one summer in the early 1970s, when I was reading about Ruth in the Bible. It intrigued me how she gleaned the fields for food. At that time, Jim and I had been living on faith for about five years. I had the idea of asking God to lead me to someone with a garden. I would ask them if I could glean the garden for the leftovers they did not want. I had canning jars and knew how to can, so I planned to put up food to help us in the coming winter months. I was surprised that I could not find anyone with a garden who had leftovers and that God had not answered my prayers.

The summer came and went. In September, we received a phone call from a prayer group in Ohio that we had ministered to. They told us that they had something to bring down to us because God had laid it on their hearts to plant a garden for us that summer. The seven couples planted the garden, tended it, and brought us a year's supply of canned green beans, tomatoes, and corn, plus potatoes, onions, home-made pickles, and a side of beef. God had abundantly answered my prayers more than I could possibly imagine.

Another time, God graciously provided Easter dresses for Cheryl and Heather. Because we were living on faith, we did not have a clothing allowance, but had to trust God for any new clothes. One year, Easter was coming, and I happened to be cleaning out the closet on the landing between the second floor and the attic. In the closet, I found a paper bag full of dresses for little girls, including two lavender organdy dresses, a size two and a size four. They had beautiful smocking on the front, long puffy sleeves and large bows in the back. They fit the younger girls perfectly for Easter dresses and Teri already had a nice dress to wear.

I didn't have any idea where the dresses had come from and had not heard of the name brand. Months later, when I was shopping with my mom, we found a small shop in Lexington that carried the same name brand. When I talked to owner of the shop, I learned she had the only shop in Lexington that sold that brand of dress. The owner said that she only sold one size of each dress of each style. God had provided us with two exclusive designer dresses in my daughters' sizes, the only two sold in Lexington.

The bag also contained enough dresses to clothe Cheryl for kindergarten that fall. God never stopped surprising me with His provision. I hadn't even prayed for new dresses for the girls, but He knew our needs.

At Christmas time we experienced another incident involving clothing that was really funny. Jim talked to our daughters about buying Christmas gifts for a less fortunate family with some of the money we could have spent on our family. Everyone agreed to do this, so we bought the gifts and Jim and the girls delivered them to the family we had chosen.

The day after we did this, a woman in town called and told us that her family had decided to buy Christmas gifts for a family less fortunate than them. They had picked our family. A store's delivery truck brought several packages to our house. The packages contained a beautiful long paisley-print dress for me, a cashmere sweater for Jim, and gifts for the girls.

God certainly has a sense of humor! But the lesson I learned is that there is always someone with more than you have, and there is always someone with less. That is just life, so we should never be proud or arrogant because of what we have, or bitter because of what we don't have. Be thankful to God in whatever situation we find ourselves.

Closing Christ Center

About five years after Christ Center opened, the owner of the building told us we had to either buy the building or move out. By that time, most of the original staff members had moved on to doing other things. Jim was left with just a few of the original people. The rest of the staff members were people who had come to the Center for help. After praying and seeking God, Jim felt that God had given him a date to close the Center if He had not provided the money to buy the building. Jim didn't tell any other person this specific date because he wanted to make sure that what happened was according to God's plan, not ours.

About that time, one of the ladies who had been helped by the ministry of the Center came to talk to Jim. She lived in a very nice house in the suburbs and had invited the staff of the Center to her home for dinner many times. She and her husband had marriage problems and eventually were divorced. She came and told Jim she felt that she should sell her house and give the money to buy the building for Christ Center.

Several months passed, and the date came that God had given Jim. He did not tell me the date until the day after it passed. He told me that he was going to close the Center down. Soon afterwards, the woman came in and said that her house had sold. She wanted to give Jim the money, but he refused it. Jim told me later that he would not have taken the money from a single parent who needed the money herself for her family. It was a very generous act on her part and was a sign of her love and commitment to the Lord. She ended up using the money to relocate her family and start over again.

It seemed that the Lord had spoken, so we made plans to close the Center. Things were sold and liquidated and the money was given to another non-profit ministry. The board of directors decided that the money Jim and I had put in escrow for the rent should be given back to us. God had faithfully provided the money to pay the rent through donations that were given by our supporters, and ours was never needed.

Jim and I decided to try to buy the home we had been living in because the money we got back was enough for a down payment. If we were able to buy the house, we thought that it would be a good sign God wanted us to stay in Lexington. At that time, Jim could have applied to become the pastor of a church in another area. After the Center was closed, Jim and I started speaking in churches and at retreats, and leading workshops on the subjects of marriage and living by faith in God.

Next, Jim had to approach the landlord about buying the house. We didn't have to wait long because

Bill, our landlord, came over to check something at the house. Jim had asked God to give him the opportunity to discuss the subject, not knowing if Bill and his brother were at all interested in selling the house. Bill's family had owned the house since it was built in 1907.

Jim and Bill were on the roof, discussing what repairs needed to be done on the house. Before Jim could mention anything to Bill about buying the house, Bill turned to Jim and asked him if we would be interested in buying it. Jim told me later that he was so surprised when Bill asked him that he almost fell off of the roof.

Our next hurdle was agreeing on the price for the house. In prayer, Jim felt that God gave him the price we were to pay for the house. Jim told me the amount, and we started praying for God to put that amount in Bill's heart. Bill called and told us that he was having an appraiser come to appraise the house, and that we would talk about pricing then.

I was not as relaxed as Jim was about buying the house, so I told him that I wasn't going to clean the house before the appraiser arrived. I was hoping that the appraiser would set a lower value on the house. Jim laughed at my wanting to manipulate the situation and said that I must have the house extra clean.

After the appraiser came, Bill called us and set up an appointment to talk about the purchase of the house. I still remember the day when Bill sat across the dining room table talking to us. When the subject of money finally came up, Bill said that his brother and he wanted $25,000 for the house and $1,000 for the furniture in it. All of the antiques in the home were left for us when we moved in. The price of $25,000 was the exact amount the Lord had given Jim for purchasing the house, so we bought it and stayed in Lexington.

Reflections

Ephesians 3:30, "Now to him who is able to do immeasurably more than all we ask or imagine, according to his power that is at work within us, to him be glory in the church and in Christ Jesus throughout all generations, forever and ever. Amen."

God blessed us by allowing us to experience a season of His provision far above all that we could ask or imagine. We realize as we go through life that it is in His answering prayer, not just in our asking, that we see the hand of God at work in the midst of our lives. He is the giver of life and our provider.

Chapter Six

SEASON OF LESSONS LEARNED ALONG THE WAY

John 14: 26, "But the Counselor, the Holy Spirit, whom the Father will send in my name, will teach you all things and will remind you of everything I have said to you."

The Three-Ring Circus

*O*ne autumn, some time after we had moved out of the Center, Jim and I went to the Boone Tavern in Berea, Kentucky, to spend a weekend away by ourselves. We tried to get away at least once or twice a year while we were in ministry at Christ Center. One evening, we walked to the little town theater to watch a movie. Fred Mac Murray starred in a movie about a man who lived in a small town and was a Boy Scout leader. As I remember, the show was about him, what he and his sons did, and their close relationships. Jim and I both left the movie theater in tears. We realized that we both wanted to have this type of atmosphere in our home to raise our children.

At that time, we were living in more of a "circus" atmosphere with people in our home all the time, living with us and eating with us. Also, we had people come by who needed help any time of the day or night. Sometimes it felt as if our life was a three-ring circus with different situations happening in each one.

I would like to share a story about a high school-aged girl who lived with us. She was one of the most difficult cases that we had in our home. She was very hardened, angry, and rebellious during the year that she lived with us. When she left our home, we thought we would never hear from her again, and we didn't for over thirty-five years.

I received a message on Facebook in 2010, asking me if I was the Dixie Parker from Christ Center. I answered yes and asked the person who she was. The person responded, Gina. I wrote back that I didn't know anyone by that name and she replied that her real name was Regina, but she went by Gina now. I couldn't believe what I read, realizing who this person was. She continued to share that she wanted to thank me for all that I had done for her and she shared her testimony with me. She has given me permission to share it now. Regina wrote:

As a young child I remember having a love for the Word. I would sit for hours reading my Bible. I had such an understanding of the Word. I didn't have a good relationship with my mother. She had re-married and he was not a nice person. He raped me for years until I ran away from home. My heart had become hardened. I was angry and bitter. I trusted nobody, not even God.

In my seventh year of school, I had a Christian teacher. She introduced me to her friend, Dixie Parker. Dixie and her husband Jim and their friends had started a place called the Christ Center, coffeehouse and all. They had a heart for the lost. I happened to be one of the lost. Jim and Dixie took me into their home. They spent countless hours praying and ministering to me. They loved me and fed me. They made sure that I went to school. Dixie tried so hard to nurture me. I just would not give her or anyone a chance to help me, let alone trust God, someone I couldn't see or touch. I can remember many nights at the Center with them praying for hours over me. I just couldn't receive. I was too rebellious. I knew what they were saying was truth because I once had a love for the Word of God.

The day I left their house, I had no idea where I was going. I was lost and desperate. At that point, I didn't care. Yet I had the Word in my spirit. Scriptures that Dixie had quoted to me so many times would come to mind many times a day. Eventually I ended up pregnant. The baby was stillborn the following year. Still, I could hear Dixie saying, "Regina, Jesus loves you. He has a plan for you."

Then I met a lady who was ten years older than me. I lived with her for about seven years in a homosexual relationship. During that time, I still had the Word rising up in me. It was God saying the Word, saying this is wrong. I started drinking to numb the pain and the conviction. For twenty years I lived like that, into drugs and alcohol. Still, I was living either under guilt, or condemnation, or conviction.

God always planted a Christian in my life along the way. I had met a couple of people who were Christians and started to attend church. Still active in the gay lifestyle, still at times taking drugs. I could still at times hear Dixie say, "Regina, Jesus loves you."

Then one day someone at church was talking about some Christian counselors they were seeing. I went home and I shall never forget that in my spirit I heard, "Here is your chance. Call these folks." I was cleaning my bathroom and I heard it again. It was on a Tuesday night in late November. I went into the kitchen and called. Understand, it usually took weeks and sometimes longer to get an appointment.

But the following Thursday I had my first appointment.

I remember when I got into the counseling room, one of the counselors said to me, "Regina, do you know Jesus loves you?" I wept because I knew that Jesus had held and protected me all those years. And yes I knew He loved me. I was still a wounded soul, hurt, bitter and angry. But I knew Jesus loved me.

I went to counseling for seven years. I took anger management classes, a healing of damaged emotions class, and co-dependent classes three times. I was a slow learner (had a hard time with making amends: Chapter 9.) But my life changed and my appearance changed. I hadn't worn dresses since high school. I had to allow Jesus to give me my identity. I had lost my own identity. I loved it. I loved to shop for pretty dresses and heels and handbags. I learned to love Jesus, to know *Him*, and not just know *about* Him. I could go on and on.

We had loved the ministry we were part of, but were realizing that things had to change for our family's sake. Jim and I knew that our main priority in God, after our relationship with Him, was our family. But it wasn't easy to make our family a priority while living in the middle of so many difficult life situations.

I realized that I really did want to have the time to be a Girl Scout leader for Teri's Girl Scout troop.

I wanted to have the time to be actively involved in raising our daughters. A child's life is like a diamond, with many different facets, but each facet is beautiful and makes the diamond sparkle. I didn't want to miss even one part of their lives.

A lesson I learned during this time was that if I was too busy when Teri came home from school, she didn't talk about her day. I realized that she wouldn't intrude on what I was doing, if I was talking on the phone or something else. She would just go to her room. I prayed and asked the Lord what to do and He showed me. When it was time for Teri to get home from school, I would set the stage. I would be sitting in the back yard drinking a glass of iced tea, appearing not to be busy.

When Teri came home that first day and found me not busy, she sat down with me. After I asked her how her day went, she almost talked my ear off. From that day on, I always tried to plan my day's schedule so the atmosphere was set up for sharing and listening about Teri's day in school. I wanted our children to know that they were important in our lives. I had to show it in my actions, not just in my words. Teri was in junior high school, which is a difficult time in every-one's life. The lesson I learned through this was the importance of letting the children know that they were a priority in my life.

I remember the story of a teenage boy who we met through the coffeehouse ministry and came to visit us regularly at the Center. One day, he was telling us in tears that his dad had just bought him a new car, but what he really wanted was for his dad to just spend some quality time with him. Instead of spending time with him, his dad would just buy expensive gifts for him.

One evening in the coffeehouse, I was sitting at a table with a cheerleader squad from one of the high schools. We started talking about the girls' relationships with their parents. I was amazed at the comments the girls made. Several said they felt that their parents didn't really love them. When I asked them why they felt this way, they told me that their parents didn't really care what they did. Because of that, they didn't really feel they were loved. They went on to tell me that if their parents really loved them, they would be concerned about what they were doing and would set boundaries for them.

Another parenting lesson I learned is that proper boundaries make our children, no matter what their age, feel secure and cared for. As our children grew into adulthood, we continued to sit together and go over the boundaries for our family life

Learning Contentment

I would often argue with God over how He did things. I can remember once when Jim and I were asked to speak at a state convention for a women's ministry called Aglow. After speaking, we went back to our hotel room, and Jim went to bed.

Instead of being thankful and content with the ministry God gave us, that night I lay on the hotel room floor, sobbing over why God had made me only an ordinary clay pot and had made another couple we knew as beautiful vessels. I was not satisfied with what

God was doing in my life as long as I was comparing myself with others. Instead of being thankful for my life, I was jealous and grumbling about someone else in ministry. Whenever I compared myself to another person, I never felt that I measured up.

When you compete, there is a winner and a loser. Instead of being secure in Jesus and using the Bible as my guideline for my emotions, I used emotions and looked at things from a purely human perspective.

In our natural way of thinking, if twenty girls are trying out for places on a cheerleader team and six are chosen, then six are "accepted" and fourteen are "rejected." Or, if two people apply for a job, one is "accepted" and the other "rejected." In God's plan, however, it's not that way because everyone is important to Him and He provides for everyone and rejects no one.

Another couple had joined our ministry team. We had different gifts, and God used us in different areas of ministry. Jim and I loved the inner-city ministry with the children and adults in Davis Bottom and Irish Town. I was immature and thought that we all should be doing the same thing, my way. Inside myself I started secretly competing with the other couple.

The Bible says that God is not a respecter of persons—He has made a place for each of us in the body of Christ. He isn't partial to one person over another. We have been specifically designed and created for a particular job. No one else can fill our place in the body of Christ. We are all needed.

I realized that when God uses someone else to do something, it doesn't mean He is rejecting me. It means He has someone else designed for that particular area, and I need to be doing what He designed me to do. There are no winners and losers in God's plan. He has a place for us all, and we each have a job to do.

I had to learn how to look at life God's way and let Him renew my mind to have His perspective on life and not mine, which was guided by pride. I was trying to be God and tell Him what to do instead of letting Him be God and being content to be His servant. Again, I was reminded that no one wins in a standoff with God.

I can remember once that I was struggling with the way God was doing things, and some things weren't happening the way I wanted them to. God gave me a view of the situation in my mind's eye. In the late 1940s, my brother and I would go to the movies to see Roy Rogers, who starred in movies about cowboys and Indians. Sometimes, the Indians would catch a cowboy and torture him by staking him to the ground, spread-eagle over an ant hill.

One day, God showed me that I was at war with Him. I saw myself staked out on the ground spread-eagle as in the cowboy movies, but I wasn't over an anthill. Even though my body was tied down, I was still lifting my head off the ground and arguing with God.

He said, "Dixie, when are you going to quit struggling and do things my way?"

That day, I realized that no one wins in a standoff with God.

Whenever pride is leading me in my actions, I am at war with God, because the Bible says that God resists the proud and gives grace to the humble. When I want to do things my own way instead of God's way, pride is leading me. In my cowboy and Indian vision I was raising my head up, saying, "But, but, but!" to God.

When I saw this picture of myself, I realized how silly and futile my situation was. I wasn't going to win. My pride was so ridiculous—thinking I could win in a standoff with Almighty God, maker of heaven and earth. I needed to have God's perspective of life. The Bible had to be my standard for my life, not my emotions or feelings.

While cleaning houses one day, I experienced God's sense of humor. I have told you how I have battled with pride during my lifetime. For twenty years, when I owned and operated a house-cleaning business called "Mini Maids," I cleaned bathrooms. On the days that we cleaned six houses, I did eighteen bathrooms. That meant that I was staring into eighteen toilets a day while cleaning them.

One time, while driving to a house to clean, I was following a BMW sports car and thought, "I could have been that lady driving that car and I could have someone coming to clean my house." Instead I was the one doing the cleaning. I laughed and told the Lord I wouldn't change my life for the world. My life—with God, Jim and our girls—was worth more to me than anything I had given up to follow Jesus. God had blessed us with more than we ever thought we would have. I am thankful for my lot in life.

I don't think that the women whose houses I cleaned could quite understand me, because I always wore my diamond rings and didn't take them off to clean. Sometimes, my diamond rings were larger than theirs, yet I was cleaning their houses. Many times I got to share my testimony about my relationship with the Lord while cleaning. For two years, I had a Bible study in my home for some of the women whose houses I cleaned. They would drive up to my home in a Mercedes or BMW while I drove an old station wagon.

I realized that true hunger for the Lord and His ways is the same in all people. Hunger for the Lord has nothing to do with who we are, what we have, or what we do. God made us all for fellowship with Him and we won't be satisfied until we are in a relationship with Him.

Reflectors of God's Love

Another lesson that I have learned along the way is that God wants me to be a reflector of His Love. When I look into the mirror, I see the reflection of myself, but God wants other people to see in me a reflection of His love. Instead of seeing me, He wants them to see His love. Through my actions, the world can see the love of God expressed in human form.

I have gone through seasons when God has had to change my perspective of life and give me His perspective, so that I could be a reflection of His love to others. God has had to change me so that I could be a reflector of His love. I had to realize that love is something that God is, and not just something that He does. Why does God love me? It is not because I am always lovable, but because He is love and cannot keep from loving me. He loves us no matter what we do. We don't have to "try" to get Him to love us.

Most importantly, I never want the fact of what Jesus did on the cross for me to become "old hat." I never want to become complacent about how Jesus expressed His love for me in His death on the cross. I want to always be consciously aware that God loves me. His love for me is sacrificial love to the highest degree. Jesus was the greatest example of someone who reflected God's love. His ultimate reflection of love was when He gave Himself to be crucified for our sin.

Before I became a Christian, I did not instinctively know how to love with God's agape (unselfish) love. After I became a Christian, God started to teach me how to live life His way and how to love with His love instead of my own love. My own human love is very different from God's love. He loves me with agape love, which is undeserved love and doesn't depend on how I perform, how I look, or how perfect I act.

When I was living at Christ Center, God first taught me the difference between my own love and His agape love. I came to the end of any capacity I had to love people in my own ability. When a child would put their arms around me, and his or her head was full of lice and I hugged them back, it was not my love doing it. When I would go into a house and have to excuse myself because I got the dry heaves from the stench of body odor and human feces on the floor, only God's love could cause me to stay and extend a helping hand and show love for the people.

Another lesson I learned along the way is that many times it is harder to love our own family with unselfish love than it is to love outsiders. We had just moved from Christ Center into our home on Transylvania Park when I took Cheryl, who was then two years old, grocery shopping with me for the first time. Cheryl and I never had been grocery shopping because we had lived at Christ Center since she was born.

The day we went shopping, I had a grocery list and a certain amount of money to spend. As we went up and down the aisles, my daughter Cheryl wanted everything she saw. For example, Cheryl wanted every kind of cookie on the cookie shelf, which is pretty normal for most two-year-olds. I bought a small box of cookies, but that didn't seem to appease Cheryl, so she kept on asking for things.

The farther we went, the more irritated I got, because I was trying to watch the amount of money I was spending and felt under a lot of pressure. It is interesting that I didn't feel under pressure when we were praying for our food and money to live on, but I did feel under pressure when I was grocery shopping with a set amount of money to spend. Anyway, my tone of voice got more and more curt and irritable.

When we arrived home, my friend told me how upset she was about how I had talked to my daughter and the tone of voice I had used. If I was an example of a Christian mom, she didn't want any part of it. As my friend spoke these words, I felt as if someone had thrown a bucket of cold water in my face. The Bible says in Proverbs 7:6, that the wounds of a friend can be trusted. I took to heart what my friend said, and I repented to the Lord and asked Him to give me His patience and love as a mother, and to give me His unselfish love for my daughters.

Loving unselfishly also includes talking to our spouses in a respectful way. God showed me one time, when I was angry with Jim and telling him what I thought, that I needed to treat Jim as a brother in the Lord first. I would never have talked to someone at church in the tone, words, or attitude that I was speaking with Jim. I had given myself the liberty to speak harshly to my husband and children. I needed to talk to my husband as a brother in the Lord, and to my daughters as sisters in the Lord, as far as respect, tone of voice, and so on. I should not talk to them any more disrespectfully than I would a friend or prayer partner. I had to repent of my lack of love and ask God to give me His unselfish love for my family.

Needless to say, learning to love unselfishly is something that I have had to learn again and again. Life sometimes is like an onion. There are many layers to life, and just because you get through one layer doesn't mean there are not a lot more left. I keep reminding myself that I am in a process and God won't be finished with me until I take my last breath here on Earth. I will never be finished with the process of God dealing with me to make me into the image of His Son. Years ago, I asked someone just why God doesn't deal with our carnality or flesh all at once.

They replied, "Because it would probably kill us."

Out of His love, God changes us a little at a time. When I repent of being selfish and ask God for forgiveness, God replaces my selfishness with His unselfish love. I exchange my imperfection for His grace to live His way. God saves each person for eternity at one point in time when he or she becomes a Christian, but the exchanged life goes on for the rest of our lives. I have had to learn the lesson of loving my family with His unselfish love many times.

Blind, Deaf, or Brain-Damaged?

I learned a lesson about receiving God's love from others, when I was forty-four years old and became ill with tubercular meningitis. At first, I was a patient at O'Connor Hospital in San Jose, California. At O'Connor, I was the first person whom they had seen with the disease in thirty years.

I can remember lying on a gurney cart just after I was admitted to the hospital, knowing that something was very wrong with me and thinking, "God, I don't know what is wrong, but I do know that You love me."

I was determined not to fall into the trap of thinking that God did not love me because something bad was happening to me. As human beings, we are tempted to feel that God loves others more than He loves us when life seems easier for them.

When our friends and the people from my church heard about the seriousness of my illness, they began to pray earnestly for me. I am convinced that what kept me from dying and enabled me to recover as a normal person were the prayers of our friends and the people from our church who prayed twenty-four hours a day in thirty minute shifts until I was released from the hospital. In His time, God answered their prayers by healing me.

After five weeks at O'Connor Hospital, I was in constant pain and still wasn't improving. Then many of the people fasted (gave up whatever God told them to give up, such as meat, desserts, and so on) for a week. At the end of the week of fasting, intense prayer, and seeking God, three people told Jim they felt God had impressed them that I was to go to Stanford Hospital.

When Jim saw my internist the next day, before he could mention to her about moving me to Stanford Hospital, she told Jim she felt I needed to be moved to a teaching hospital. She thought a teaching hospital would be more aggressive in my treatment. Stanford was one of the choices, and God made it possible for me to be transferred there.

When I got to Stanford Hospital, I learned that four people in California had contracted tubercular meningitis that year. I was the only one who survived. The neurologist at Stanford told my family that if I did survive, I could be left blind, deaf, or brain-damaged, and possibly all three because I had such a severe case. He called doctors in India, who had treated more cases of the disease, to talk to them about the correct way to treat me.

I was at Stanford Hospital for only a week when I was well enough to be released to go home. The neurologist at Stanford took the advice from the doctors in India and doubled the dosage of my medicine and it worked. While at Stanford Hospital, one of the neurologists took a video tape of me to use for teaching purposes. He also took another tape after I fully recovered that showed that I was not left blind, deaf, or brain-damaged.

After being released from Stanford Hospital, it took me two years to fully recuperate. I still don't understand why I was ill for two years, but I do know that the Lord sustained me. I survived the disease and came out with normal eyesight, normal hearing, and normal brain functioning. Although I was in great pain when I was in the hospital, that part of my life now seems like a dream.

Here Today, Gone Tomorrow

Another miraculous healing happened to me during this period of my life. Jim, our two youngest daughters, and I went to Bass Lake for a week's vacation. At that time, I was going to Stanford Hospital once a month to be checked out by my neurologist to make sure I was progressing properly. I had a CAT scan every few months to check my brain, because tubercular meningitis is a disease in the meninges, the covering of the brain. I had several MRIs and CAT scans during the time I was hospitalized. In fact, I had a CAT scan the day before we left for our vacation at Bass Lake.

Our cottage on Bass Lake didn't have a telephone or other conveniences, but it did have a great view of the lake. On the fourth day of our vacation, we found a note on our door after we returned from swimming and enjoying the sun. It was a request to call my neurologist at Stanford. My doctor later told me that it had taken him several days to find me because I was not at home and didn't return his calls. He finally checked my files and found the phone number of my mother, who lived in Kentucky. He found out from her where we were and how to reach me.

I nervously called the doctor and was shocked at what he told me. He said me that the CAT scan had revealed an aneurysm in my brain. I asked him how big it was and he told me. I also asked him in the next breath, how big aneurysms usually were when they could burst and hemorrhage. He told me that mine was already that size. He also told me that the chief of staff of surgery would be waiting for his call when I arrived at Stanford. By now, it was already evening, so there was nothing we could do until morning.

Jim and I were in such shock at the news that we had a hard time accepting what it could mean. I lay awake all night, unable to sleep because I kept thinking about a pregnant woman in Oakland who had unsuccessful brain surgery. It had been in the newspaper, because she was left brain dead by the surgery, but the hospital kept her body functioning on life support until her baby was born. All I could think about was the fact that, if the worst happened, I could die or be left with brain damage and be unable to function.

The next morning as Jim and I were in the bathroom, I could only tell Jim that I couldn't sleep all night and then I became quiet. Jim asked me if I needed to talk about what the doctor had told me and all I could do was nod my head. At that, Jim took me by my shoulders and faced me toward him. He looked deeply into my eyes and told me that he had been thinking all night and wanted me to know that, whatever happened, he would always take care of me—no matter what state I was in. We both started to cry and we just stood there, holding each other.

After talking with our daughters, we drove back to the San Francisco Bay area, and I went straight to Stanford Hospital. The doctors immediately did a test where they put dye into the blood vessels leading to my brain and took an angiogram. They wanted to determine how large the aneurysm had become and its exact location before doing surgery.

Even though we followed the advice of the doctor and went to the hospital, we were depending on God to help us. People from our church had started praying as soon as we called and told them what the CAT scan had revealed. They continued to pray while I went to the hospital for surgery. The test done by the Stanford doctors showed that my brain was free of aneurysms. There was no longer an aneurysm—it was totally gone. All we could do was thank the Lord for answered prayers.

God is God. He is so powerful that He could have healed me instantly the minute I was diagnosed with the disease. However, that is not how God chose to do it. He was with me through the two years that it took me to totally recover. A lady asked me what God had taught me from having the illness, and all I could think of was that I had survived and was thankful to be alive and able to hear, to see, and to think normally. I was not left with any deafness, blindness, or brain damage, which is what they had expected.

Another lesson I learned through this experience was to trust God with my life. I also got over any fear of pain that I had. God's grace was there for me through the whole traumatic experience. I had always thought that I was afraid of dying. However, I realized it wasn't the fear of dying, but of the pain you can feel before you die, that I feared.

During my illness, I had experienced extreme pain, but the grace of God was present through it all. In 2 Corinthians 12:9, Jesus says, "My grace is sufficient for you, for my power is made perfect in weakness." I found that the Scripture was true in my life. God's grace is sufficient for whatever situation or circumstance, whether physical, emotional, or mental that I go through or find myself in.

Princess Do-It-All

There are a lot of lessons that I am still learning along the way. One is that God loves me and accepts me for who I am, not for what I do. It is so easy to become a Christian workaholic doing God's work, especially when you love the Lord and think this is pleasing to Him.

During a season of time, three of my close friends and our adult daughters went backpacking and hiking one week every year during the summer. Each year, we picked a "princess name" for each person that depicts how the year has been for that person. We picked the "princess name" at the end of the week, and the women picked each other's name, with our approval, of course. That year my friends named me "Princess Do-It-All." That name pretty much described me. It seemed like I had my hand in about every pot there was. I didn't see this in myself, but my friends did.

While we were hiking in the mountains of Colorado on a trail with wildflowers higher than my head (I am five feet, two inches tall), my friend Kim and I stopped to admire the flowers. As I was standing in the middle of these beautiful wildflowers, looking across the mountain range, I felt God spoke to my heart that I should take a sabbatical for two months.

I went home and told Jim about it, and he agreed. Next, we conferred with our pastor, who also thought it was a good idea. I told our pastor and Jim it would be a three-month sabbatical. After two months, I still felt like a hamster running in an exercise wheel that spun around but went nowhere. After two months of rest, my mind still had not shut down, and I was still not experiencing the inner peace and calm that I was seeking. I looked peaceful on the outside, but inside I still felt that I was going 100 miles an hour.

I ended up being on a sabbatical for a whole year. During that time, I decided to not go back into the women's ministry. One Sunday in church, our pastor's message challenged us whether or not we were using the gifts that God had given us for His purposes. When I asked the Lord, He told me that I wasn't using my spiritual gifts and that He wanted me to lead the women's ministry council at church once again. I had to learn how to be better at delegating and let others do their portion of the ministry. Now, I try to pace myself, realizing that I don't have to do everything. Doing everything was something I was expecting of myself, but it was not from God

God has good works planned for us to do, but our task is just to be obedient to His directions and

His timetable. I had to learn what a real Sabbath rest meant. I also found out that if I tried to do it all, I was keeping someone else from doing what God wanted to train that person to do. God did not call me to be a Superwoman, but to be an obedient daughter and child of His.

To keep the right perspective, I keep reminding myself of a word picture that God gave me just after I became a Christian. God bought me with the price of the blood of Jesus. Because God owns me, He can do whatever He wants with my life, just as I can do anything I want with a dress that I buy at the store. I can hem it up, cut the sleeves off—whatever I want— because I own it. God owns me the same way. He bought and paid for my life. He owns me and I belong to Him.

Stop The Clock

God uses various things in a woman's life to process her, but I think that one of the major ones in my life has been motherhood. I have realized over the years that once a woman has a child, she is in the role of a mother for the rest of her life. This role has many different parts and the role changes as the child grows up. What doesn't change is the fact that, once a woman is a mother, she is a mother for life and that includes all the joys and heartaches involved in being called "mother."

I am now a grandmother, and my perspective on mothering has matured over the years. I have learned a lot of lessons about being a mother and about myself as a person. Both kinds of lessons have come through experiencing joy and pain as a mother.

Looking back over my life, there are many things I would have done differently, and there are many things that I would not change. However, I realize at this stage in life that the mothering instinct is just as strong in me as when my daughters were born. Now the instinct to love and protect my grandchildren is just as strong or stronger as it was for my own children. Since I am older and have lived more of life, I do not look at life quite as naively as I did when I was a young mother. I am more aware of the dangers and pitfalls that come through just living life.

When I raised my own daughters, I really thought that, as Christian parents, if we raised them with the right standards, they would not go through any hard or difficult times but would sail through the teenage years without any mishaps. How naive I was! I remember saying to one of my daughters, who had just gone through a very difficult rebellious time that was very painful for all of us, "I wish you would have listened to us and then you would not have had to experience all this pain."

Her reply was, "Mother, did you listen to your parents?"

Of course, the answer was no. I hadn't listened either. I guess we all have to learn our own lessons in life. At that time I started praying for God to protect my daughters from harm from the results of wrong decisions that they might make. I continually had to release them and pray for them.

Once a mother, you are always a mother at heart, and once a grandmother you are always a grandmother at heart. This is all to point out that, as a mother, I have had to learn to release my children to God during all the different periods in their lives. Releasing your children to God is the only avenue to having peace in your heart and in your home.

I can remember when Teri was five months old; she had a still-unknown virus that killed twenty-four babies in the Ohio Valley. For ten days, Teri was in an isolation room at a hospital in Columbus, Ohio, and we didn't know if she would live or die. Any mother who has ever held a small infant wracked with a 105-degree fever knows what I went through.

After Teri was transferred from the hospital in Mt. Vernon, Ohio, to Columbus by ambulance, I was not allowed to be in the same room with her or hold her while she was in isolation. All I could do was watch her through a large window and try to release her to the God that I didn't know on a personal basis yet.

All mothers go through fear and anxiety for their children as they grow up and fall down stairs as toddlers, as children fall out of trees, or come home late when they are old enough to drive a car. These are all opportunities to learn to release them to God on a deeper level.

When our daughter Teri moved to Africa with her husband and two-year-old son to be missionaries, release took on a deeper meaning in my life, because I knew they would be in dangerous situations. Teri's husband, Harmon, killed a seven-foot-long poisonous snake that was in a hedge where his son, Joshua had been playing with friends the day before. They were living in a village that was about a seven-hour drive from doctors or a good hospital. If a medical emergency happened, God would have been their only recourse.

Harmon is at this present time building footbridges for tribes in remote areas and is in constant danger of being bitten by a poisonous snake or attacked by bandits and so on. God is his only resource.

In each type of situation, I have had to come before the Lord and give Him my child, or their spouse, or a grandchild, anew, and release them into His keeping, knowing that God loves them more than I do and that He has their best interest at heart.

Another thing God has taught me is how to look at life in decades and not just days. When our oldest daughter, Teri, was getting married, I wanted time to stand still. I remember the situation well. We were at the church and I was standing at the bottom of a stairway. In front of me, across the church foyer, I could see my parents waiting to be escorted down the aisle. My two teenage daughters, Cheryl and Heather, were behind me on the stairs in their bridesmaid dresses, and my oldest daughter and her father were at the top of the stairs. Teri looked beautiful in her wedding gown and veil. All I felt at that moment in time was, "God, stop the clock. Make time stand still!"

I didn't want my family to change. I didn't want Teri to get married and move across the United States, and I didn't want life as I had known it to change. I realized then that in the next ten years I would probably lose a parent, all of my children would probably be married, and Jim and I would be in the "empty nest" years.

If I could pass on any wisdom for young mothers, it would be to cherish your time with your children. Look at life in decades. If your child is a young teen-ager, enjoy the time, because in ten years they will be on their own, and you can never relive the time once it is gone. I think that how we spend our time changes when we look at it this way. All of life is in seasons, and once a season is gone, it cannot be recaptured no matter how hard we want it back.

Jim and I have made it one of our priorities to spend a lot of special time with our grandchildren. I had lots of tea parties with my granddaughters when they lived close by, and lots of fun times with our grandsons playing putt-putt golf. We loved it when they would come to our house for a long weekend or a week in the summertime. Some of the most fun was when they were all here together, and we would have a huge slumber party with just Grandma, PaPa, and all the grandkids. Sometimes we would throw rules to the wind and have ice cream for breakfast if that was what they wanted! What fun!

Now that our grandchildren are adults, we try to have special time with each one, but it is more of a challenge. None of them live close by. One thing I have learned is to enjoy each moment, each day, each visit with our children and grandchildren. Since I have gotten older, I never take them for granted, and consider each one a special gift from God. I can never go back and recapture the fun I had playing with my grandchildren as toddlers, just discovering the world they lived in, or the excitement they had on their faces as they raced up the driveway to greet us with their little arms thrown around our necks. Once it is over, it is gone forever, except in our memory bank. However, tomorrow is a new day with new adventures and with new cherished moments and, because our family is spread out from Africa to California, the hugs and kisses are always there over the phone, if not in person.

The Wallpaper Disaster

Yet another important lesson I learned along the way was the value of a plumb line, both physically and spiritually. A plumb line is a tool that carpenters and other builders use to make sure the walls are truly vertical and consists of a weight hanging from the end of a string.

A few years ago, a good friend called and asked me if I could possibly help her wallpaper her husband's office.. I said it would be fun to spend the time together. Our efforts turned into a disaster.

Whenever I start wallpapering a room, I use a carpenter's plumb line to get a true vertical line before I start putting the paper on the wall. Working with my friend, I used a carpenter's plumb line to start the first roll of wallpaper. But the wallpaper had a faint line in it that made a plaid design in the paper. The walls of the room were not square, so we were trying to be careful that the lines in the design matched in the right places. We wallpapered for about eight hours and stopped to eat dinner.

After dinner, we eagerly got back to work putting up the border so we could finish the job and admire our work. We gasped in horror as we put the first strip of border up! Everything looked fine at first. But when the border was put up, the room appeared to slant! Although we had matched the lines in the pattern of the wallpaper, we had very slowly gotten off the true vertical line from the plumb line. The wallpaper looked terrible, and nothing could be done to remedy the problem.

My friends had to hire a professional wallpaper-hanger to redo the room. Nothing could be salvaged, so they had to buy new paper and start all over again. The professional wallpaper hanger explained the problem. With the type of paper we were using and with walls that weren't square, we had to drop a plumb line every two feet to keep the edges of the wallpaper truly vertical.

The Bible is my spiritual plumb line, or standard, in God. God's standard is the Christian's standard for life and how we live our lives. However, I can't use God's plumb line just occasionally, the way I used a carpenter's plumb line just once when I was wallpapering the room with the plaid paper. I have to use my spiritual plumb line constantly throughout life by reading the Bible frequently and comparing my life to the standard of God presented in the Bible.

In the Bible, in the book of Amos, it says that God dropped the plumb line on the nation of Israel to measure how they were doing in following the ways of God and to see where their passion for life was coming from. God did judge them for being half-hearted in their walk with Him.

If we don't drop the plumb line in our lives or have an ear to listen to God when He drops the plumb line, we are in danger of becoming just as slanted and off-balance in our lives as the wallpaper in my friend's home. The wallpaper became slanted so slowly that we could not see our error until we tried to put up the border. If we don't judge our lives by God's plumb line, we can slowly bend farther and farther away from His standard, and our lives will eventually not match at all with what He wants.

A. W. Tozer wrote in 'The Pursuit of God', "They try to walk the tight rope between two kingdoms and they find no peace in either. Their strength is reduced, their outlook is confused, and their joy is taken from them."

As a Christian, my goal in life is to have a heart devoted to God and to serve Him with all of my being. As I measure my life by God's plumb line and follow the guidance of the Holy Spirit, I will be changed more into His likeness. "More of Him and less of me" is my heart cry.

Master of The House

I have been tested and tried these past months (2014) on who is the master of my house (my life) as far as my thought life is concerned. One morning when going to the bathroom, I notice blood in the toilet. The rest of the day, I noticed blood every time I urinated. I was not feeling any pain, so I tried to ignore the blood and see if it would stop. By four in the afternoon, I told Jim that I thought I needed to go to the ER to find out what was happening. After a CAT scan and many test, the ER doctor told Jim and me that there were only two choices of what my diagnosis could be, given my age of seventy-three years and the fact that I wasn't having any pain. I either had a urinary tract infection or I had bladder cancer.

We were shocked at the prognosis, but I told Jim I was not going to relate to the fact that I could have bladder cancer until we had all the facts. I know that God's grace is there for truth, not for a fantasy or the "what if's." I had to exercise self-control over my thoughts to keep them in line with what we knew the truth to be. I needed to go on the facts, not the emotions I was feeling.

Tuesday morning, the doctor called to say that the test for the urinary tract infection came out negative, so I had to wrestle with the other option, bladder cancer. I called Cheryl, our daughter who is a nurse in an ER, to get her advice on what to do at this point. Cheryl advised me to call my regular doctor. I called my doctor and he told me he would call the uroligst immediately and ask him to call me. The urologist called two hours later, and while talking to me, he looked at my CAT scan results on his computer. He immediately found the solution to the problem as he saw two 6 mm kidney stones in my kidney and one was at the opening, causing the bleeding.

In the past, I would have related to the "what If" and would have my death and funeral planned out in my head. In past circumstances, I have spent so much emotional energy on things that never happened except in my thought life. If something was a possibilty, I would take it to the farthest point in my thoughts and emotions and be exhausted by the time the truth was known. In most situations, I wasted all the emotion and energy relating to it for nothing. When I talked to my pastor about the situation with the possiblity of having bladder cancer, we agreed that if the truth was bladder cancer, God's grace would be there for me through the process.

Reflections

Well, here I am at almost seventy-four years old, and I am still in the learning process. My hair is grayer, my face has wrinkles, my body moves slower, and I walk sometimes with a limp from two knee replacements that left me with a knee that is less than perfect.

Am I finished learning all the lessons in life that God wants me to learn? Of course not! God will have me in the process of growing in my relationship with Him for my entire life. He will continue to change my life, and mature me, but His grace will be there for me when the hard times come. And they will, for this is how life works. My story will continue on, and I eagerly look forward to more lessons learned along the way, because it is these life experiences that teach me more about Him, His love for me, and His mercy and grace available to me.